FINTECH

How Financial Technology Is Predicted to
Change in the Major Levels

(The Critical Legal and Regulatory Challenges
Confronting Fintech Firms)

Mack Austin

Published By Mack Austin

Mack Austin

Fintech: How Financial Technology Is Predicted to Change in the Major Levels (The Critical Legal and Regulatory Challenges Confronting Fintech Firms)

ISBN 978-1-77485-402-0

Legal & Disclaimer

The information contained in this book is not designed to replace or take the place of any form of medicine or professional medical advice. The information in this book has been provided for educational and entertainment purposes only.

The information contained in this book has been compiled from sources deemed reliable, and it is accurate to the best of the Author's knowledge; however, the Author cannot guarantee its accuracy and validity and cannot be held liable for any errors or omissions. Changes are periodically made to this book. You must consult your doctor or get professional medical advice before using any of the suggested remedies, techniques, or information in this book.

Upon using the information contained in this book, you agree to hold harmless the Author from and against any damages, costs, and expenses, including any legal fees potentially resulting from the application of any of the information provided by this guide. This disclaimer applies to any damages or injury caused by the use and application, whether directly or indirectly, of any advice or information presented, whether for breach of contract, tort, negligence, personal injury, criminal intent, or under any other cause of action.

You agree to accept all risks of using the information presented inside this book. You need to consult a professional medical practitioner in order to ensure you are both able and healthy enough to participate in this program.

TABLE OF CONTENTS

Introduction

The term "financial technology" (Fintech) is a brand technology that is designed to automatize and enhance the provision and use of the financial services. Fintech can be used to aid businesses or business owners as well as consumers with managing their financial processes, operations and daily lives using special software and algorithms utilized on computers and, in the last few years smartphones. Fintech could be a mix with "financial technological."

Understanding Portfolio Management

As fintech was first introduced in the 21st Century, the term was initially used to describe the technology used in the back-end systems of the established financial institutions. Since since then, there's seen a shift towards more services that are geared towards consumers, which has resulted in a definition that is more consumer-focused. Fintech now covers a variety of industries including education fundraising, retail banking, engineering, non-profit as well as investment and financial management. Fintech is also responsible for the development as well as the usage of cryptocurrencies such as bitcoin. While there are many of news stories about bitcoin, the conventional banking system is the one with the biggest part.

The idea is applicable to the way people conduct business, beginning at the time of the invention of digital currency up for double entry. This includes things like transfer of money, deposits to check accounts via smartphones, online apps in raising money to start-ups as well as investment management and many more.

Considerations to make prior to investing

A common feature that of fintech startups is the fact that they're created to challenge or challenge and eventually, take over traditional financial service providers by becoming more active, catering to under-served segments, or by providing better and faster service.

In the past, financial service institutions provided a variety of services within one umbrella. The range of these services included a wide range of services, from traditional banking services to mortgage and trading. Fintech can provide these services in separate products. Combining streamlined services and technology allows firms that use fintech to become more efficient and cut down on transaction cost. Disruption is the term that describes how the fintech revolution has altered traditional banking and trading, financial advice and other products.

This book provides a solid base for anyone who doesn't have any idea about the current technological revolution. It can be helpful for people, companies, educators and research institutes, policy makers and the CEOs of any private or public sector company.

Chapter 1: Financial Technology Trends

The banking sector can no longer ignore its most significant current challenge the issue of technology for financial transactions. Although it is not a new idea, the term "financial technology" is a term used to describe small businesses that provide limited retail payment services, or online lending. It's now entering the mainstream and has begun to be household names.

The goal of financial technology is to provide efficient and affordable financial services that draw an increasing number of clients. Traditional lending companies must take action to stop this rise in interest for these companies in financial technology.

The financial technology startups are dominating the credit rating and money transfer online lending. They have created automated advisors that offer solutions that are based on the customer's objectives and risk tolerance. A few innovators have invented a novel method of data collection and sifting it to check the activity of traders and spot fraud.

There are three different ways established banks can respond to this threat by companies in financial technology. However, these aren't the best response. Some financial institutions employ the wait-and-see strategy and are at risk since they won't be ready if the threat is imminent.

A few banks also acquire companies in the field of financial technology so that they can profit from the new technology. However, the majority of them have integration issues. There are also institutions of finance that invest their time and resources in making sure that their IT infrastructure is able to adapt to the latest developments. But, they often are entangled in their interests along with regulatory burdens outdated infrastructure.

What is the best way an Financial Institution Can Succeed with Financial Technology

First, the business must be a thriving hub in the financial technology ecosystem. Instead of using outdated methods and outdated systems to handle customer service It has to demonstrate its credibility to customers by ensuring that they are in compliance with regulations and rules, and also by allowing access to the customer's data.

The financial institution should look into technologies for financial services with the aim of identifying new products they and their customers can make use of. Instead of utilizing resources to study and develop in-house solutions, the business could evaluate third-party technology providers. It is able to select applications and software that are compatible with the business of its clients and integrate with the supplier's systems rapidly.

The focus should be on the institution's strengths, and the use of cutting-edge technologies and products to grow its market. This implies that the bank needs to change its mission and brand to one that is constantly adapting to new technologies in order to be able respond to demands of customers more quickly.

The financial institution should be able to create new capabilities that can analyze new technologies on a regular basis and determine which ones to incorporate to the architecture of its information technology. This includes efficient collaboration with other companies and gaining insight into customer preferences and gaining managerial skills to be able to adjust to new technology and better ones, and reverse prior integrations, and also aiding in the integration of new technologies.

A second issue is that the established bank needs to adjust its high-brand and metrics for service to guide its choice of items and offerings. It's hard to switch to a new business model. The wrong handling of financial technology integration can could damage the reputation of the company. Customers are generally unhappy when a bank integrates new products and technologies quickly since employees and customers must learn more.

So it is imperative that the financial institution set up credible metrics as its primary guidelines for evaluating the latest technologies. It must be able manage interactions with customers. Being bold in responding to the challenge of financial technology is achievable. It requires focus, making plans, as well as establishing positive connections with financial technology disruptors.

Top Financial Technology Trends

Increased Cooperation and Refinement in Technology

The latest tools for financial technology are the most popular choice for investors. Prior to this, just professionals had access to customized software. With the advent of companies in the field of finance technology that even ordinary investors can utilize these tools.

Furthermore, the general public has begun to trust these startups in financial technology, that are able to bridge the gap between early adopters and the innovators. The public is paying attention to financial technology and are embracing it quickly. Companies that use financial technology are thriving by focusing on user interfaces, efficiency and effectiveness. Banks work with disruptors to bridge the gaps.

Robo-advisors Virtual Reality, and Artificial Intelligence

Since the cost of traditional advisors is costly and robo-advisers are a good choice for investors and traders who do not have high-net-worth clients. The use of videos is also a huge trend since young professionals have a very short attention spans. The efforts of disruptors in financial technology focus on the production of video.

Algorithms also disrupt the traditional exchange traded funds. Tools for wealth management online and expert advice are focused on strategies that utilize technology to make managing wealth simpler and more convenient. Open source applications remain in use.

The importance of Big Data

Big data is essential in the financial market. The availability of big data is advantageous for investors who are able to follow trends to understand and gain insight from an automated and actionable market intelligence. Datasets are becoming more sophisticated and finance-specific software makes use of these datasets to uncover powerful insights for investors, allowing them to make informed decision-making.

The Emergence of the Share Economy as well as Alternative Products

There are alternatives to traditional finance options which are currently in the radar of mainstream. The awareness of equity crowdfunding and peer-to–peer lending is constantly growing. The government is currently updating its rules to allow investors to take advantage of these new products.

Alternative lenders are much more noticeable. They also work with traditional lenders. This collaboration will change the traditional offerings and lead to models that are driven by technology, such as loans and insurability.

More Automation

Automation comes in many types, including speeds of execution, management software scanning software, Black-Box trading platforms. It makes it easier to use different applications. Many investors take part in markets because of the technology which improves the transparency of information as well as creative interfaces.

The Initial Public Offerings for Financial Technology Innovators

The desire of investors to invest in IPOs is evident today. Certain companies might go public and others, in particular those with low capital may be unable to succeed.

Security Management

Due to the advancements in payment technology as well as mobile banking the need for security management expands at a rapid pace. Fintech disruptors are continuing create innovative products, backed by the necessary security technologies to work smoothly.

Regulation Changes

Governments are currently proposing new rules to cope with the rapid advancements brought about by innovators in financial technology. Certain changes are significant to the business. This is why it's essential for disruptors as well as innovators to be prepared for the introduction of new laws.

The adoption of Blockchain

The payment across borders is instantaneous and much faster. Blockchain technology is embracing innovation thanks to blockchain technology and the complexity in international banking. Blockchain technology can provide the ability to be accountable. Financial transactions are more secure and secure. With open source applications or data feeds gets popularity as a tool for quicker payment processing across the globe.

More Internet Connectivity, Mobile Expandion and Mobility

Connectivity allows anyone to trade information, exchange data, and connect at any time and wherever. There are technology options that allow this to be done. Financial institutions can integrate with third-party solutions to offer a range of capabilities to customers.

Mobile technology is having an influence on the way the investors and traders conduct business. Applications that are well-designed are swift. Additionally mobile payments are being accepted by the majority of people. It is easier for people to transfer money nowadays thanks to these mobile apps.

Chapter 2: Banking and Financial Technology

Many businesses are employing technology to conduct business in the financial services sector. The technology revolution is impacting the way people save and invest, as well as how they store money, make loans, pay save, and even take out loans.

The year 2015 saw around 800 new financial technology companies all over the world. At present, there are around 22,000 companies in the field of financial technology all over the world. Over the last five years, companies in the field of financial technology increased to an estimated $23 billion in venture capital and growth equity and this number is growing every day.

Yet, traditional institutions remain important in the world economy. They are tightly controlled and have the sole right to taking on risk and credit issuance. They also act as the principal depositors for customer deposits. They will continue to be the main gateways to payment systems. But, the landscape has changed.

The banking system was hit with the most severe blows due to the crisis in finance. Many customers lost trust in banks. Due to the increasing popularity of smartphones, there's no longer a need to deal in person with bank branches. Smartphones are now the latest payment instruments. Customer service can now be fully personal. Additionally, data that is transparent is now accessible worldwide thanks to the dramatic reduction in cost of computing power.

Keys to Financial Technology Successful

Businesses in the field of financial technology have high rates of failure even though the present situation is not as bad as the previous dot-com boom. However, startups in financial technology which focus on retail markets can achieve success and be sustainable companies. They can transform certain areas of the financial service sector.

Companies in the field of financial technology can challenge established retail banking companies in consumer finance, mortgage and managing wealth, retail payments and SME lending companies. They are able to lower costs and reduce margins.

In securing customers cost-effectively

The companies in the field of financial technology have to develop customers from the ground up. It could be expensive, as banks already have them. They need to be able to improve their gross margins and reduce the costs associated with customer acquisition. They should look for ways to acquire customers in a cost-effective method.

For instance, there are companies in the field of financial technology which capitalize on disruptions to speed up the replacement of point-of-sale cycles. They make use of the distribution of other merchants who have connections with customers of point-of-sale systems in order to draw customers to become their customers more quickly and efficiently.

Reduced Cost of Service

Many financial technology disruptors have taken advantage of the loss that physical distribution has caused. Certain of them have cut the cost benefit since they don't have to pay the expenses for physical distribution. Customers can get significant advantages regarding processing time as well as the costs associated with loans.

Using Data Innovatively

A lot of financial technology pioneers are currently looking at new ways to improve to credit scoring. Even though most of these tests are not successful but advanced analytics and large data may provide an opportunity to identify the best option to offer financial services through new technologies like wearable devices as well as mobile phone. These techniques can also assist lenders in understanding consumer wants more.

Financial institutions' credit underwriting relies heavily on precedent and operates with a legal mentality. Financial tech startups could lead to novel methods of providing new services and products.

The Proposal of a Particular Segment to revolutionize

The most successful financial technology startups are not looking to transform the banking or credit industries completely. They typically pick one area and concentrate on the area. They usually pick a market which they believe will be more open to their offerings and services.

For instance, a financial technology company could target young professionals who don't want to incur high costs and prefer to use automated software. A different company could focus on home buyers who are looking for low-cost mortgages that are quick to approve. Financial technology disruptors typically concentrate on the unbanked as well as small businesses and young professionals as they favor low-cost transactions and remote delivery and distribution.

Making the Most of Infrastructure

Many disruptors of the financial sector become successful due to their acceptance of the existing ecosystem of finance industry. They collaborate with the existing financial institutions. They establish relationships with banks, by helping those who aren't banked, or small-sized enterprises while the banks provide loans.

Controlling Regulators and Risk

Financial technology disruptors are bound to be able to attract the interest of regulators when they begin scaling. They'll face a challenging to get past if they don't be attentive to regulators at the very beginning of their activities. Regulators are extremely strict in their conformity to various laws. Therefore, companies in the financial technology sector should ensure that they set up their business for success.

Regulation is an essential element in the effectiveness of a technology-based financial disruptive force. It influences the scope and speed of business operations. There is a possibility of an urgent need for stricter regulations in the event that the disruption is significant. Furthermore, the effects of innovations may vary between countries due to the different regulatory approaches. For instance, certain Asian countries have more stringent regulations. The regulations on the use of data differs among EU countries.

In order to be successful an organization in the field of financial technology must be able to combine these factors to build a model that can be sustainable and adaptable dependent on the competitive factors and revenue drivers.

Crucial Digital Signals

Established financial institutions could be prone to panic and overreaction due to the increasing financial technology the current flurry of activity. The markets are optimistic regarding technological advancements and a large amount of money is being poured into technological advancements in finance. Mobility is an additional game changer. Banks need to be able make the most of what is happening if they are to remain relevant in the future of digital technology.

Utilize holistic data-driven analytics to gain insights

Today, disruptors of the financial sector make use of analytics and data to address issues such as customer service cross selling and credit provision, customer acquisition as well as customer loyalty and retention. Due to the massive amount of data available banks need to be aware of the different ways the financial technology industry's innovators utilize assets, capabilities and expertise.

Banks can establish an ecosystem of data within their company to gain access to various customer information and build an effective infrastructure for data and analytics. They should create an all-encompassing overview of the activities of consumers and utilize various methods to drive scientific decision-making.

Design an integrated, well-designed and segmented customer experience

Instead of implementing a universal distribution system, banks must make use of mobile devices as well as the preferences of their customers to use real-time and cross-channel services. They should employ an attractive design to provide their services to provide an experience that is different for the customer. They need to realize that banks are not the only ones who have a direct influence on customer expectations today.

Banks need to be flexible to customer experiences that are not conventional and continuously meet ever-changing expectations of customers. Customers expect immediate transparency and access to data. They need their balances available whenever they need them. Banks need to be able to differentiate themselves and enhance the cross-channel and cross-product experience.

Develop capabilities around Digital Marketing

Today, banks are competing with banks and other non-banks for the right to acquire a client. Online retailers have an advantage over traditional banks. Big data and advanced analytics capabilities are the basis of digital marketing. To be successful banks must be capable of mastering digital media, control the lifecycle of digital customers, as well as master the art of how to integrate digital marketing and content marketing operations. It will require a large amount of money and time to establish these capabilities.

Use Process Digitization, Rapid simplification, and streamlining aggressively

After making crucial processes accessible electronically, banks now have to digitize their processes. The dot-com boom was when they converted paper documents into PDF files that could be processed easily and sharing across departments. In today's digital world it is necessary to create and alter data fields in an extremely automated manner in the cloud. This process can take years to complete because they will need to connect various platforms and systems.

Opportunities to streamline, simplify and digitization exist throughout the banking industry. Banks should take advantage of these opportunities in order to are able to be competitive with the financial technology innovators. They can utilize new technologies for testing and scaling to find efficiencies.

Utilize the latest technologies quickly

Banks need to be able utilize mobile technology since consumers are eager to connect with their devices. They also need to improve their internal processes and cultures to safeguard the data of consumers from attacks from outside. Due to the speedy acceleration of technology banks must remain ahead by creating software that is agile and has continuous delivery.

Then there is the emergence of processing and storage technology which are cost-effective. Banks need to make use of these technologies and eliminate their old technology as fast as they can. They must build modular technology layers to replace their outdated systems.

Rethink the concept of Decision Rights and organizational structures

The organizational chart of a bank typically is comprised of channels and products as well as physical distribution. The owners of the channel and product typically have the power to make decisions. These owners are usually the targets of disruptors in the field of finance, that focus on customer metrics which are related specifically to the financials of their business.

However the ethos of the culture of banks is based on consensus, so it takes time to establish an alignment. Banks employ strategies that permit them to adjust to changes in the external environment faster. They also promote environments that allow for making decisions quicker. In this way banks must structure their decision-making rights and structure to facilitate the analysis and use of data to create an exceptional customer experience.

How do you deal with challenges within Bank as well as Financial Technology Partnerships

Technology is changing the face of the financial sector. However, new businesses are confronting major hurdles to compete with established banks.

Inadequacy of understanding

Banks have established guidelines and procedures, but new startups in financial technology are developing. Therefore, knowledge gaps are common. Banks are finding it difficult to connect with their counterparts in the field of financial technology.

To solve this problem Financial technology companies organize events where banks representatives are able to look into the world of financial technology. It is also beneficial for each party to not call each other competitors. Rivalry hinders the progress of both technology firms as well as banks.

It is important to focus on strengthening and addressing the distinctive qualities of each partner. Startups in financial technology and banks should also be able to work together to provide more robust and more seamless products and services to the consumer.

Problems with Pace and Velocity

The financial technology startups are swiftly because they need to thrive by providing a quick response to market demand. However established banks operate at a the slower pace since they have the approval of their own and they are massive.

To overcome these challenges banks can learn from the financial technology startups who offer customized services to meet clients' specific requirements in banking. They can concentrate on catering to the needs of their customers with less specific tools. They could also partner with a finance technology company to use these tools.

Financial technology companies are able to operate at a rapid pace and can provide services and products quickly. Banks however need to foster innovation inside their own teams. They can also have self-managed teams, which operate in a different way and are run in tandem with companies that provide financial technology.

Insufficient Collaboration Strategy

The companies that offer financial technology don't have a clearly defined strategy to collaborate with banks that are established. They are primarily focused on their services and products.

To overcome this issue companies in the field of financial technology can overcome the gap by working with hubs which are non-profit business organizations that serve as an intermediary between the two parties. Hubs for finance help in bridging the gap and boost awareness for smaller businesses. They also help facilitate collaboration within the business.

Chapter 3: Robo-Advisors , and Wealth Management

Robo-advice utilizes automation and digital methods to build and manage the portfolios of investments. It's now a cult phenomenon and is constantly gaining recognition within the industry of wealth management. But its market share remains tiny, but it has a lot of potential because it's more affordable than traditional advisors.

Robo-advisors are part of the market segment that is not well-served. Discount brokers advocate the recourse to robo-advisors for another possibility to provide advice. But, they'll still utilize conventional advisor models which promotes direct involvement. Full-service advisors can also utilize the robo-advisor for their smaller accounts. They also utilize them to boost their efficiency.

Robo-advisors can also provide certain benefits for insurance businesses. They increase the involvement of these insurance companies in wealth management and allow insurance agents to concentrate on sales. Overall, robo-advisors will be permanent and have a massive impact on the provision of advice.

Robo-Advisor Potential

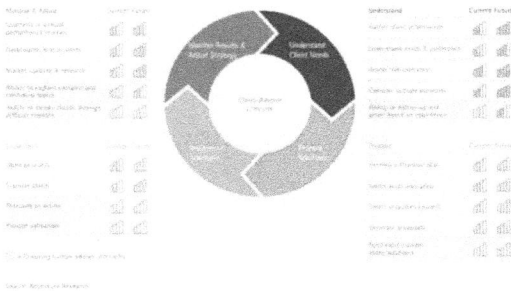

Robo-advice is a basic service. It assesses customers using easy questionnaires to determine their needs. It suggests, alters it implements and adjusts the asset allocation strategy for a specific client based upon its assessment. It also monitors, rebalancesand monitors and produces reports on the portfolio of the investor.

Robo-advice combines various steps in setting up an investment bank account. Recently, it also allows you to transfer assets. To sum up, it offers different services at a competitive cost to ordinary and new investors. It's not a good choice for investors with more complex needs.

Innovation, competition, and new ideas will enhance the potential of robo-advice greatly. Future applications will consider the various aspects of an investor. They could benefit from different objectives like estate planning health care and long-term needs security needs as well as planned home purchases, retirement savings and college. They will offer investment options that encompass all assets.

Robo-advice is able to provide education and other information to customers to help them understand their portfolios of investments better. It may also provide privacy and also allow investors to determine their own direction based on the information he has learned. Technology advancements are likely to enable the development of more robo-advice tools.

Human Intervention and the Need for Human Intervention

Many investors will prefer relationships with friends and family. A relationship between a advisor and a client is essential for investors. In general, it's essential for these investors to have someone who is trustworthy to be a source of comfort in bear markets. They want their advisors to convince them to take a choice by presenting the different options to them.

Due to the need for an individual approach it is recommended to integrate robo-advice features into the experience of a client advisor. Robo-advice is a great way to enhance and strengthen the advisor-client relationship.

The Impact of Robo-Advice on the Wealth Management Business Model

Robo-advice is a good option since it's reasonably efficient and cost-effective. Investors do not have to pay for advice on investing. Traditional financial advisors have be able to demonstrate they provide the best value and have better performance.

The people who are able to hire financial advisors to are doing so because they trust them. They believe that their personal advisors will help them build wealth. Although many investors prefer face-toface interactions, robo-advice may offer innovative capabilities to complement the firms that manage wealth.

What can Robo-Advice do to make Robo-Advice successful?

Instead of replacing financial advisors, robo-advice could help their services. Large corporations can design their own solutions, while corporations may acquire existing robo-advisory firms. Smaller companies may offer their services, or partner by partnering with a brand.

Robo-advice can be used by novice or average investors with basic needs. It's cost-effective, so traditional financial advisors need to consider their fee structure in order to remain in the game. Even with a fee structure that is low businesses offering robo-advice must try to retain and attract customers.

Achieving the Right Price and Technology

Companies offering wealth management must not just choose the best technology, but also determine the type of experience they intend to offer their customers. They must decide on the type of service they offer as well as the qualifications of investors who are able to avail of the robo-advice.

In addition, wealth management companies should also take into consideration pricing. They must determine whether to provide robo-advice as an independent product, an a basic product or as an addition to other offerings.

The Most Effective Distribution Methodology

Investors who are not traditional are the ideal audience for the robo-advisors. Young people don't have much money to invest. They are content with one or two investments to begin building wealth. Therefore, they use robot advisors to help them understand how to invest.

Companies that manage wealth must decide whether they want to develop their own robo-advisor, work in partnership with an existing robo-advisor firm or even offer robo-advisor solutions by a brand new company in financial technology.

Incorporating Robo-Advisor Services

Companies that manage wealth should come up with ways to integrate robot-advisory capabilities into their offerings and services. For instance an investor might want to speak with someone in person. The business must decide if it is better to allow this investor to speak to a financial adviser or a member the robot-advisor team.

A robo-advisor is not able to do much. It is unable to explain complex subjects in investment. It's not able to provide answers to questions. Additionally, it is not able to provide recommendations based on an investor's responses. However an investment firm may use a robot advisor for its smaller accounts , so that its financial advisors are able to focus on the more experienced and large investors.

Chapter 4: Big Data and Financial Technology

In the last few years, large data had seen rapid growth. It has opened up numerous opportunities for the analysis of unstructured as well as structured data. Companies use big data to gain valuable and useful information to aid their managers make better decisions. Health care, financial services marketing, technology, and other industries rely on big data.

Without the use of big data analytics, businesses could have a hard time gaining competitive advantage. In financial services, large data is crucial in providing more information that aids in making investment decision. Algorithmic trading makes use of large amounts of data coupled with mathematical models to increase the profits of investment portfolios.

Big Data Concepts

The three fundamental features of Big Data are the speed quantity, variety, and velocity. Banks have the ability to discover new methods of using technologies to help make their business efficient, despite the growing customer demands regulations, as well as increasing competition. Financial institutions rely on big data to gain advantage over competitors.

Velocity refers to the speed of the storage of data and its analysis. Financial institutions can take advantage of this as a advantages in competition by emphasizing rapid and speedy execution of financial transactions.

Big data may be either unstructured or structured. Structured data is information that is managed by the company in relational databases or spreadsheets. Unstructured data is information that has not been organized without pre-defined data, like social media data.

Due to the increasing the volume of data banks must be able to effectively manage data. Asset management firms as well as investment banks need to utilize massive data to make informed decisions. Insurance and retirement firms benefit from the massive amount of historical information to control risk in a proactive manner. Banks and financial markets have to be able to manage ticker data in a proactive manner.

Algorithmic trading can be described as an automated method that executes investment trades at speeds and frequencies that no human being could ever imagine accomplishing. It allows trade executions and in the most convenient places , and at the highest prices. Automation allows you to lower the amount of errors that humans make because of their behavior.

Financial institutions are able to use algorithms that use large amounts of data to test strategies and make educated decisions. They can discern valuable information and eliminate low-value data. They are able to create algorithms that use both unstructured and structured data. Robo-advisors employ algorithms and large data.

However, the financial service sector is still facing many difficulties. There is always worry about privacy issues relating to the methods of collecting unstructured data. Additionally, data analysis requires advanced statistical methods. In some cases, spurious correlations can arise solely through random chance.

The algorithms usually identify potential opportunities for investing in the long term using the historical data. It's difficult to create effective results that are able to are in favor of short-term investment.

Big Data Expectations

Information technology plays a crucial role in not just business, but also in daily life too. Since the late 1970s with the advent of personal computers, users today are able to access mobile phone as well as gadgets. They have the advantages and disadvantages of the digital revolution.

Pension funds and asset management could have been challenging to manage with computers and software. But, there are issues with standards and regulations. There are also shady individuals and companies that have access to the systems. Cyber security is now an issue for banks and financial institutions.

Due to the advancement of technological advances, managers of assets must to present their assets in detail in order to stay in the game. In lieu of Microsoft Excel, they have use programs which are more advanced. Endowments and pension funds require lower costs and more ways to invest of fund management. Fund managers therefore need internal systems that provide aggregation and transparency.

Regulations are becoming more strict. For institutions that deal in finance they have new rules and regulations that can be burdensome and expensive. Financial managers must prepare the appropriate reports electronically and according to a schedule. Before, banks could would outsourced certain tasks, while maintaining their own infrastructure. Nowadays, they are able to outsource all back office tasks.

It is also essential to secure personal and proprietary information. These instant messengers are very popular. Employees can communicate with one another as well as with clients via these systems of communication. Providers must make sure that the platform used for messaging is safe.

Asset managers are extremely cautious when it comes to using cloud services because of cyber security concerns. They fear that unscrupulous organisations will take their concepts. Additionally, investors aren't confident in cloud services due to hacking attacks.

However, times do change. Cybersecurity is a topic that has gained a lot of confidence. security and protection. They also know about the growing popularity and influence of the social web. They are therefore able to the idea of having personal data stored in the cloud. It's also great that they are now aware of the regulations of the world.

Thanks to technological advancements, it's now more simple to conduct research. It is much easier to discern the latest trends, allowing people to make better choices. In the past investors only learned about a macro-level shift within two years. Nowadays, they are able to detect trends in real-time. In the same way, businesses can easily track their competitors thanks to technological advancements.

Chapter 5: Crowdfunding and Peer to Peer Lending

Crowdfunding

Other financial instruments are essential in the advancement of technology for financial transactions. Crowdfunding is the process of connecting people who want to contribute money to support a particular project on the internet. For lending and equity big institutions are taking over once more. Unfortunately, these businesses are now financing or directing these programs. Thus, crowdfunding has turned into an overused term.

Financial technology began in the 1950s, as Lyons Corner House Tea Shops began computerizing ledgers. Lyons created one of the very first computers for office use in. Today, financial technology encompasses funds, investments and funding as well as transfers and payments. New currencies that are alternative are more convenient and easy to conduct transactions online. Yet, the offline usage isn't well-known.

Since the introduction of online transactions and payment using alternative currencies, banking is becoming costly and ineffective. With crowdfunding, anyone can become angel investors for companies that are starting. In the present, more and greater people trust the companies that are pioneers in financial technology since they provide better and more efficient solutions and products.

The financial technology startups could perform the majority of banks' functions if they are able to offer a secure, intelligent and clear network in a cost-effective , quicker manner. Since the network is impervious to corruption the majority of customers are able to trust the financial technology innovators.

The decrease in intermediaries led to the democratization of currency and finance.

This is actually advantageous to the people because it creates a level playing field. For the majority of financial institutions, it can be extremely difficult. Technology in finance can cut down on intermediation, increase the accessibility of financial and banking services and lessening inequalities and inefficiencies, as well as friction.

Established financial institutions might have a difficult time reinventing themselves , since doing so would cost money. Customers can also be demanding, since they have the ability to see their power due to the popularity on the web. They seek streamlined and simple products that are easy to access and use.

Crowdfunding can help entrepreneurs grow their businesses because they can raise funds for their business from people who support their cause. Businesses can flourish without bank loans because of crowdfunding.

Utilizing Financial Technology to facilitate Crowdfunding

Crowdfunding is launching the new era of. Many people are aware of its benefits and benefits. Entrepreneurs benefit from crowdfunding when they need to raise funds for an upcoming launch for their new product. On the other hand investors make use of crowdfunding as another method of diversifying their portfolio.

The current small and medium-sized companies also consider crowdfunding to meet their financial needs. The companies might require money to expand their operations or purchase new equipment. They might consider crowdfunding as part of their efforts to launch new ventures or expand their current operation to other countries. Crowdfunding allows entrepreneurs to reach their goals. It is possible due to the fact that the platform is that is provided by the financial technology.

Transferring funds online is now more convenient thanks to the advancements in the advancements in financial technology. At first, financial technology enabled people to keep track of their financial transactions but only. It later offered the possibility for consumers to use credit cards for making purchases on the internet. Presently, crowdfunding utilizes this technique to provide the entrepreneurs with financial aid through the pooling of funds from individual investors.

The financial technology also allows access to a variety of gadgets. Users can utilize any gadget they own to manage their money. They are able to perform different functions without having to appear personally at an institution. With a smartphone they are able to make reservations and purchases. Additionally, investors may decide to invest in a crowdfunding venture with their devices. In contrast entrepreneurs are able to manage their projects using their own devices too.

Customers are more comfortable with transactions on the internet due to advancements in technology in finance. They make use of the platforms more often to conduct financial transactions such as banking, shopping and other financial transactions such as crowdfunding.

Peer-to-Peer Lending

Peer-to-peer is a term used to describe two entities which interact without the requirement of an intermediary. Computer networking is a type of network in which computers can connect to another without having to use a central server connection. Internet is peer-to -peer network.

Users can directly connect with others on a social network to exchange games, music pictures, videos, and other content. Peer-to-peer connections can be an impact either positive or negative on the user, based on their perspective and experience.

Benefits of Peer-to-Peer Loan Platforms

Peer-to peer lending companies have increased their business over the last few years. In comparison to banks, these disruptive businesses have lower prices and could continue to gain significant market share.

Peer-to peer lending leverages modern technology, allowing entities are able to communicate with each other directly. Advantages competitive to this type of lending include higher returns for creditors and lower costs for debtors, availability of credit to customers who are not served by bank loans; the ability to provide greater and more accountable social impact; and the utilization of technology to enhance speed and efficiency of service.

The higher return on loans was due to peer-to peer lending platforms have the advantages of cost compared to banks institutions. Administrative and overhead costs are extremely low. Peer-to-peer lending doesn't have an interest margins when it is matched by the debtors and creditors. However, lenders are more at risk since this type of lending doesn't guarantee returns or deposit insurance.

Peer-to peer lending also provides an increased accessibility to credit. Banks and traditional lenders are less likely to provide loans to debtors due to the financial crisis that has hit the world. They are required to meet certain criteria for approval of credit. Peer-to peer lending is an additional option for small companies as well as individuals who want to borrow at a much lower rate.

Peer-to-peer lending connects individual debtors and creditors and provides financing in a socially-friendly way, without taking advantage of market power or seeking to make profits which do not consider the interests of customers. In addition, it makes use of technology advancements, so peer-to peer lenders are able to provide superior services to both debtors and creditors.

Peer-to-peer lending uses technology in two ways. First, the auction method connects the borrowers to the lenders, with the borrowers providing the most interest they're willing to pay to get the loan. The lenders will also provide the interest rate they're willing to pay in exchange for their funds. The system matches the borrower to the lender.

In addition, the lending platform will match the lender and borrower with the current market interest rate for the risk class. This kind of arrangement could result in delays due to the fact that there could be more debtors than creditors or debtors with more creditors than lenders. The interest rate is adjusted as time passes to accommodate the imbalances.

Chapter 6: Harnessing and Using the Potential of Automation

Because of the enormous amount of financial data industry the importance of automation has grown in traditional banks as well as startups in financial technology. Artificial intelligence converts data into valuable information needed by investors in order to create significant returns.

The financial algorithms employed by robo-advisors generate the investment portfolios of their clients without human intervention. Financial planners worry that they'll be soon losing their job due to the advent of the automation. These robo-advisors currently manage approximately $20 billion worth of assets in the world. The experts believe that the automated advisors will soon manage at the very least $13.5 trillion in investments in the near future.

Additionally the blockchain ledgers and cryptocurrency are becoming increasingly popular. Artificial intelligence robots write as well as sign Smart Contracts. They can easily validate and communicate transactions. Automatization is a way to legitimize financial transactions that involve cryptocurrency. Many experts believe that the virtual currency will be legal in the near future.

How can the Financial Industry Prepare for Automation

The mortgage industry is prepared for the automation. The processes in the mortgage industry are ready for the transformations brought about by technological advancements in finance. There are processes in place to simplify the outdated practices for collecting customer data and processing of home loan applications.

Automation could trigger changes to financial services. Experts believe that established banks could be forced to lay off at least 2 million employees over the next 10 years due to of automation. Technology and new competitors are set to compete with traditional lenders. These developments can help employees more efficient and precise in carrying out his work.

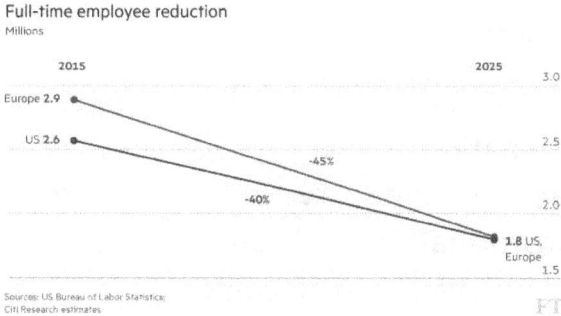

Full-time employee reduction
Millions

	2015		2025	
Europe 2.9				3.0
US 2.6				2.5
		-45%		
	-40%			2.0
			1.8 US, Europe	
				1.5

Sources: US Bureau of Labor Statistics;
Citi Research estimates   FT

Automated the loan applicant is able to simply submit his application with all the necessary documents in less than one hour. In the past it could take several days to finish the application procedure. Due to the automation process, there is no requirement employees to gather and enter the applicant's information into a computer program. This means that the process of approving loans becomes quicker.

Automation may free employees from mundane tasks so that they can better provide service to customers. For mortgages as well as trade finance employees could be fired because automation has already done their work for them.

The Reasons Financial Institutions must automatize business processes

First that, business processes are becoming more inefficient and costly. Financial institutions need to consider automation since it takes a lengthy time to complete manual tasks. Automatization software vendors are competing on the market, and companies may have a difficult time choosing the best software for their requirements.

There are several automation software providers which can tailor the application to fit the budget and requirements of the financial institution. They can meet with the management team to discuss options that are most appropriate to the requirements of the company.

The second issue is the an absence of integration, which takes some time to finish the current process. There are automated systems which do not work with the legacy systems of banks. There are however, good systems that work well with the existing systems. Automating business processes can cut down the time needed to complete tasks. Additionally, a reputable automation service provider will provide additional assistance.

For instance, an insurance company has to handle at most 22,000 invoices, which require minimum 70 persons to take care of. Five different individuals must review each invoice prior to payment processing begins. The entire process can be time-consuming and the movement of paper can cause documents to be lost during the process, which could lead to delays in payment. Automating the process can cut down on delay and the errors that occur when processing invoices.

Thirdly, employees are focused on manual work when they are required to complete other tasks that are crucial. Automation of business processes leads in increased efficiency of staff because it cuts down time doing tedious work. This improves morale of staff and productivity as employees are able to make use of their time and talents in tasks that are more crucial.

Fourth, software is able to automate manual processes only. It's always the responsibility of the person who is responsible for the process to manage the entire business process. Many believe that automation is not flexible and is not able to meet the specific requirements of a company. However, this isn't the case. The process owner is able to give his input before allowing the software to continue to run the process.

Fifth, human error wastes lots of time and money. Automating manual tasks can be difficult for staff members initially. Training employees could be difficult because it requires time and money to switch from an outdated method to an automated one. However, automation simplifies business processes. Financial technology disruptors can combine platforms and systems to simplify everything.

Sixth, large-scale process issues could require large-scale solutions. Automation will depend on requirements of the business processes. It is possible to automate the smallest but most critical procedure. So, employees will become familiar with the system.

Seventh, the necessity to automatize business processes could be a matter of opinion since automation is a decision that relies on the requirements of the company. Additionally, automation should fit in with the visions of the business and business plan. The advantages must be far greater than the time and cost to implement automation. So, some businesses may not need it.

Key factors to realize the need for automation include flexibility, efficiency, as well as scaling. The purpose of automation is to increase efficiency across the company.

Chapter 7: Financial Technology Startups Going Public

In its initial public offering valued at $5.4 billion, which was listed on the New York Stock Exchange, Lending Club started a new environment where innovative entrepreneurs can participate in what was previously an exclusive financial sector. The market for financial technology is estimated to be worth billions of dollars. The increasing number of investors are beginning to take notice of this area.

There are many innovative financial technology companies waiting to begin their ventures with their first public offerings. A few of these businesses are catering to small and student-run businesses as well as individual consumers. There are also companies that concentrate on special loans such as commercial franchises, mortgages or business loans. Lending Club's IPO of Lending Club was an initial step in the direction of a structural change in lending credit to small-sized businesses as well as consumers.

Going public is not an assurance of success particularly in the business of lending. In 2008 the US SEC required Prosper and Lending Club to close their doors as regulators devised ways to monitor the activities of these innovators in the field of financial technology. As per some analysts Lending Club was able to beat its competitor due to its ability to solve the problems of regularly.

Lending Club was stricter with its lenders and borrowers since the beginning. However, Prosper relied on the pure market method in its business. Both of these pioneers of lending faced challenges with regulators. The year 2008 saw Bay Partners revived Lending Club with new money.

Over the years, payment businesses have received lots of attention and financing. They have a variety of potential and real financiers. But, these online lending businesses need to be public if they wish to gain money and expansion. The regulators do not permit using equity in the expansion of these lending companies.

In addition, the lending economics makes online lending more lucrative as compared to the other types of finance. It is a risk to lend money, and lenders earn more profit from it. In the past, financial technology innovators would think of going publicly traded. In the present, the majority of them would like their businesses to remain privately-owned.

Recently, the companies have been negotiating privately for a huge valuation. They have raised billions of dollars therefore there is no need for them to become public. There are fewer companies in the field of financial technology that are listed on stock exchanges in the US. Due to market volatility the idea of going public has become less appealing to the innovators.

But, a lot of financial technology companies are preparing to list their businesses once markets begin to stabilize. While there is a lot of an increase in demand, the valuations for startups aren't that great so it's ideal for startups to hold off.

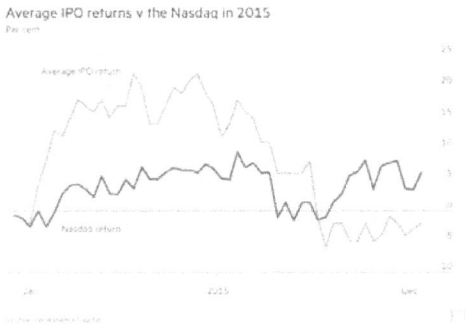

Average IPO returns v the Nasdaq in 2015

In the end, startups in financial technology will be listed on the market because they can increase their visibility through listing. They'll become legitimate even though they're small. Management can earn money by selling stock. Employees are able to sell their stock on the stock exchange. Visionaries of financial technology recognize that they will only ensure their company's sustainability through public offering.

However the public offering also implies that investors have the ability to examine the books of the firms. Investors in public companies must see quarterly financial results, which means that companies need to show that they are profitable. However, as these companies are risky analysts, bankers and market watchers are skeptical of these businesses and their faith. In the end, the market will be stabilized.

Number of US-listed tech/internet IPO deals slump to post-crisis levels

A lot of financial technology companies discovered that they could be secret while raising a large amount of cash. In the past, rules were not allowing companies to be private when they had reached an amount of investors. Today, investors invest their money into companies in the field of financial technology through private agreements because they get higher returns.

Issues with the valuation of Startups

Since fewer startups in the field of financial technology were able to go public, it has made it hard for the investors evaluate the true value of high-value startups. In the second quarter of 2015, just 50 companies in the financial technology sector were listed on the stock exchange. In 2016, experts aren't expecting more companies going public.

A lot of these startups are merging , so investors face a challenge in valuations. Most of the firms are not worth it on paper. Private companies have high valuations and some have valuations of more than $1 billion.

However, many financial technology companies which went public have an undervalued valuation compared to the initial price for public offering. Venture capitalists have difficulty to find the most reliable estimates of valuation.

Chapter 8: Managing Security in Financial Technology

Financial services need to keep up-to-date with most current security and cyber-security threats. They need to equip their business with better security. But, the financial technology disruptors are constantly evolving due to the threat.

These companies in the financial services industry must make sure that they evaluate their security policies and tools regularly. To ensure that their software is secure it is essential to have a variety of IT controls to ensure multi-layered security. This is crucial since no one tool can be effective in tackling security risks.

There are devices which combine a variety of security capabilities within one device to safeguard web-based client services as well as web servers. These capabilities include content filtering for web sites, virtual private networks (VPNs), firewalls malware, anti-malware, as well as the detection and prevention of intrusions. They are all important in all IT environments so combining all of them in one device is cost-effective and performance-centered.

There are solutions that blend diverse security capabilities, however they're software-based. The apps are available intended for devices such as tablets, notebooks and desktop computers, as well as smartphones. The security options for endpoints include firewalls, anti-malware, and intrusion detection and prevention. They reside on the device, not on a network.

Server add-ons, or dedicated devices can detect harmful or suspect content in emails and internet traffic. These devices also guarantee the flow of traffic is efficient. In the present, in addition to cyber-attacks on websites as well as attacks by malicious email.

Financial institutions have to secure sensitive information when they send it via unprotected networks. However, they should discover ways to protect information stored in storage. They can make use of enterprise-wide encryption solutions. These encryption tools differ based on the type of storage.

There are several financial technology companies which offer a range of options for authentication products. These tools are hardware- or software-based. They are able to support web security and give users access to a variety of authentication methods, including biometrics, smart cards or cryptographic tokens. They decrease the chance that an attacker could obtain credentials and then reuse them.

Financial Technology Innovations for Security Management

The financial sector is one of the first adopters of technology advancements since they ensure the safety of its customers as well as provide numerous opportunities. Digital technologies can benefit financial services and can open new avenues to connect with various channels , including social media and mobile users.

However, these technological advances also make financial institutions vulnerable to risk. Cyberattacks are commonplace in the banking industry and can target important information.

There is a huge demand for IT infrastructures and networks. But, there is an increase in the number of intelligent security threats. It is essential to have an integrated solution that uses centralized security management, and simultaneously making sure that there is complete transparency in the operation. Financial institutions can profit by the advantages of an integrated and powerful security management system.

A reliable security management system provides integrated security. It should protect the entire system and devices from dangers using one platform. Presently, no platform offers complete automated security measures. Therefore, a reliable platform needs to be able automate certain elements of managing security. Cloud-based security provisioning and other repetitive tasks could be an element of the automation. Security management should be part of cloud-based infrastructure.

To ensure that operations are efficient for efficient operations, it is essential to have an organized security policy that is segmented to ensure security is operational. This involves assigning routine tasks of configuration to different groups to ensure that the security team can concentrate on incident responses and surveillance. The challenges in security management increase when there isn't transparency in the detection and responses to incidents.

It's hard to protect and monitor devices when it is difficult to observe the security settings. Security personnel must first comprehend and visualize the surrounding environment, so that it is aware of what normal behavior. In addition, full spectrum visibility lets you automate even-sized responses and allows a better understanding of the potential risk.

More Tough ISO as well as IEC technical Report for Better Risk Management

The financial sector is increasingly using mobile banking , electronic banking services, as well as open networks. This means that it is facing new security challenges due to threats such as malware attacks, phishing, and cyber-attacks. It has to be able combat these threats by having a solid security management system that safeguards financial and consumer information.

This IEC as well as the ISO Technical report offers more support for the financial industry to establish the right security management platform to provide its products. Additionally, this support helps customers feel more comfortable with the business.

The ISO/IEC Technical Document 27015 offers security guidelines for services that support of the management of security of financial and processed information assets. It is a supplement to with the ISO/IEC 27001 standards on security systems. ISO/IEC 27002 is used as the standard of reference in all industry.

Financial institutions are the most obvious targets for attack. Additionally, they have a unique risk profile. It is crucial for them to secure the financial and customer data in order to ensure a high degree of confidence. This report ISO/IEC Technical Report 27015 offers additional security guidelines specifically for financial services to ensure that financial institutions can take care of the risks to security of information.

Chapter 9: Regulating Financial Technology

The Office of the Comptroller of the Currency of the US Treasury Department asked financial tech startups to think of methods to control their sector. Some companies asked if OCC could offer breathing room to allow them to develop and test new ideas without risking sanctions from the regulator and being subject to legal actions.

The financial technology startups do not seem to be naive in the need for more compliance. There is an increase in third-party relationships with banks, particularly in the application technologies in the banking industry. This means that it is necessary for more regulation. Banks and financial technology companies recognize that there needs to be an incubation time for both to evolve.

Companies in the field of financial technology are making a comeback on

Wall Street with blockchain technology and social networks, algorithms and mobile phones that are able to eliminate traditional banks. The rise of these startups gives the prospect of using advanced technology to improve the financial system to make transactions more efficient and more efficient.

Certain economists view the use of technology in finance as a solution to financial system issues like opaqueness, lack of competition, high operating costs, high complexity and a lack of business culture. In reality, they were confident about the financial revolution fifteen years ago.

Today, due to the rapid pace of financial and technological development it is necessary to regulate the financial technology sector. Regulators are unable to maintain the speed of this sector. Technology has the potential to change things within the system of finance to improve it. It is equipped with tools that improve the financial system by making it more efficient, transparent, and secure.

Finance is distinct from other sectors because it is governed by a legal framework. Banks earn revenue by lending money to their customers. They are exposed to risks of liquidity. There could be the possibility of a bank run or a panic in the banking sector if a large amount of depositors take an immediate withdrawal, making banks insolvent and unliquid.

To prevent this from happening, guarantees need to be made. Banks need to perform better. However, guarantee programs can cause negative side effects due to the fact that they promote excessive risk-taking. Regulators need to be involved so banks don't become reckless gamblers, who make use of the money of other people.

Banks have to comply with regulations on capital to avoid becoming reckless with their money of the depositors. However, the implementation of rules is difficult since banks are often angry over the regulations. Most often, they complain about the cost and stringent regulation procedures.

Prior to the advent of the internet it was simple for financial regulators to control the sector because regulators could oversee the balance sheets of banks. Nowadays, technology has enabled banks to make each changes to their balance sheets at a low cost and at high speed, cover all states. This revolutionized credit, making it hard for regulators to ensure strict capital requirements.

In the 1980s In the '80s, regulators introduced capital requirements which obliged banks to maintain at least the required ratio of equity-to-asset. Securitization was introduced by financial technology that concealed the risks from the regulators. This led to regulators revised their capital requirements. They introduced second-generation capital requirements which let capital requirements be contingent on credit, operational, and market risk.

The new rules did not perform because the regulators failed to examine what financial technology could accomplish. Bankers could use a variety of options to bypass capital requirements. The risk distribution covered shadow banking, which transformed loans into different structures. Thanks to trading technology and electronic pricing banks were able to build a sophisticated system of transactions involving derivatives.

Aspects of Shadow Banking Emergence of Shadow Banking

Innovations in financial technology could not eliminate risk immediately. They were so complex that no one could understand these innovations now. These products could avoid regulations, deceive regulators, and enable banks to take on risk in a reckless manner.

In certain industries, such as transport, accommodation, and catering, technological advances aid in making transactions simple and clear. For the financial sector technological advancements caused the financial system to become vulnerable, opaque, complicated, and inefficient.

Regulations on banking and public guarantees are not working because banks are still finding ways to skirt capital requirements. The capital requirements of the 3rd generation are also extremely complicated. There is currently no functioning and flexible regulatory framework.

In the US the US, peer-to-peer lending connects debtors and creditors directly distributes risk in an the most efficient and cost-effective manner. However, it's already gone. Asset management companies, banks and hedge funds have taken over the investor part. For instance, Varadero Capital, a hedge fund, was granted a 150 million in credit facilities from Citi which allowed the deposit at Citi to get access to market for loans.

The investment banks are now using marketplace loans to securitize machines. They buy securities backed by assets on marketplace loans and then turn into collateral to secure loans in the money market. Banks borrow money from mutual funds insured by the government , or from banks with deposit insurance. This is similar to shadow banking between 2007 and 2008.

Solutions to the Present Regulatory Probleme

Nowadays, financial innovation can lead to repeated financial crises transparency, opaqueness, over-risk taking, and the complexity. Therefore, it's recommended to acknowledge the failures in the past as the first step in moving ahead. There is no efficient implementation of bank regulation. It's difficult to establish one since financial institutions always seek ways to circumvent capital requirements.

Since regulation of banking does not function it is not necessary to address the negative consequences of government-backed assurances. Financial institutions use technology in the financial sector to evade regulations and cause bubbles. The tax payer's money will help these banks in the event that they face another financial crisis. Removal of government guarantees can oblige banks to accept accountability for their actions.

The financial system should not be vulnerable to panics or panics and. It's fragile due to the fact that it makes money from credit, and is prone to risk of liquidity. Banks contribute to this type of fragility.

Making the most of financial technology

The debtors need massive loans. The depositors only have the smallest amount. Banks are able to pool money of the depositors and lend the funds to people who are borrowers. However, peer-to–peer lending could be used to perform this same function. There are platforms which pool funds from different people and then loan them to the borrowers.

There are a variety of methods to deal with information imbalances efficiently. There is no longer a need to say that banks must conquer these. There are platforms that can revolutionize industries. This kind of revolution could also occur in the finance sector.

It is a common belief that banks must provide liquidity. But, in the current age, online platforms offer transactions with low costs, which means they could substitute banks that provide liquidity. The digital age is liberating people from requirements of banking. It is necessary to ban on all businesses that misuse their balance sheets to make cash from credit.

The government must stop being able providing bank guarantees, as well as inefficient and expensive bank regulations. The government must permit banks to make use of the latest technology in finance and create an updated regulatory framework that is applicable to the requirements of our current times.

Sectors of Financial Technology that Struggle with Regulation

There is some confusion in the field of financial technology about the regulatory agency that regulates it. For banks, it's certain which organizations regulate them. For startups in financial technology, this isn't as certain. Additionally disruptive financial technology companies know what rules and regulations pertain to them specifically.

These regulations and rules existed long before mobile phones, e-commerce and the internet came into existence. Financial technology has introduced new and exciting methods of delivering financial services. This is why there is some doubt about the importance of such regulations and rules. In addition, many startup companies that are in the financial tech sector are challenging the concept of a complex model of regulatory compliance because they typically employ a small number of employees.

Chapter 10: The Benefits of Fintech for individuals and small Companies

The technology is used in the financial services industry that includes lending and borrowing retail banking, money transfers, mobile payments investing, fundraising, management, among others. Here are the top five advantages associated with the financial technology sector:

Better Payment Systems

Fintech could be a useful software that can help companies more accurate in the collection of payments. Additionally, they make sure they'll maintain good relations with customers, which will increase the likelihood of returning customers and new customers.

Rate of Approval

Small enterprises all over the U.S. are beginning to utilize the financial technology lending services. The biggest benefits of these lenders are their accessibility and speedy approvals for loans (typically with in 24-hours).

Greater Convenience

Many Fintech companies offer a single payment platform, for example Adyen. The Adyen Company serves quite 4,500 companies across the globe.

Adyen Fintech also features a impressive list of customers, which includes:

* Uber

* Netflix

* Spotify

* L'Oreal

* Burberry

* Facebook

* Symantec and Microsoft

The transactions are extremely convenient, they can process transactions through tablets and mobile phones. They'll only continue to expand and provide a better experience to customers.

Efficient Advice

A lot of the latest platforms rely on Robo-advice to help users in understanding their financial situation. Fintech could be a inexpensive option, and you'll gain more data using this method. The main disadvantage is that this comprehensive guidance won't come from an experienced advisor.

Advanced Security

Security methods employed by Fintech companies are extremely secure and keep the data of their customers secure. A lot of consumers utilize Fintech without regrets since it is safe to invest in. Additionally, there are a lot of options you could use, including biometric data, tokenization, and encryption.

Lower Costs

Fintech can also provide people with the benefit of having lower cost of services than traditional businesses receive. It is often necessary to push all brick-and-mortar business expenses, such as rent, advertising and salary. Instead, invest more cash into their clients.

5 Strategies Fintech Benefits Small Businesses

The first wave of fintech-related apps was initially aimed at consumers, from Robo-advisors and online-only banks to apps for saving and saving money, among others. The sector has increasingly turned towards small companies, offering smart solutions to a variety of finance-related issues. Fintech companies that focus on businesses withless than 100 employees have raked in $10 billion since the year 2013. That's an indication of the possibility of growth in the market.

What does this mean to small-sized entrepreneurs? Sure, not every Fintech is created equally. However, at the heart of it all numerous companies offer ways to automate manual tasks, gain access to customized financial services, and expand your financial operations without adding employees.

Here are five ways that Fintech helps SMBs:

1. Expansion of Finance Options

Small business owners require money to fund the growth of their business. About half of proprietors of businesses in 2018 said that they required external funding to run their businesses. Banks as well as Fintech have been trying to conquer this enormous market by offering various services ranging including traditional small business loans , equity fundraisings, the financing of small businesses based on revenue, as well as credit cards for small businesses. A sign of their efforts is the fact that they have taken a portion or all of the process of applying online, which makes it easy and easy entrepreneurs to be aware of the options available to them.

The fintech sector has also developed alternative financing options for small companies. For example, Circle Up helps commodity businesses finance their expansion through the combination of equity fundraising and credit. Startups can apply online, as well Circle Up collates interested investors. Additionally, Snap Advance offers business owners cash advances that support by a percentage of their potential sales.

2. Automating Accounting

A solid financial operation and support can be crucial components of any business and are especially important when you're a small or growing. A thorough understanding of your finances enables you to make better decisions on when and where to put your money, whether taking out a loan is a wise decision, and whether you can be able to afford the next employee. However, more than half of small-sized businesses don't have an accountant or bookkeeper. Fintech solutions are emerging to fill these gap. Although they aren't able to substitute the expertise of real-world professionals but they can help simplify the financial burden.

A variety of new online solutions offer software that handles invoices as well as payroll, accounts payable expenses as well as income forecasting. There are a myriad of alternatives for small entrepreneurs. For instance, TeamPay may be a start-up company that lets companies offer digital credit cards for employees, and monitor and approve expenditures in real time. In addition, some of the most well-known players in the field, such as Intuit which produces QuickBooks it's own accounting software, is expanding by providing even more tailored services for small and medium-sized businesses.

3. Allowing Online Payments

Payment solutions have proved to be crucial in enabling small companies to rise over the top and compete on a larger scale. Smaller businesses do not have to be restricted to accepting just a few types of payment options. It could be that payments can only be made from inside those countries are not acceptable. U.S. Square revolutionized short business transactions by making it possible for small businesses of one or two people to accept debit and credit cards with ease. If you're operating an eatery or selling handmade items and other items, you can accept electronic payments through your phone.

Other software has helped small companies to start their own low-cost websites for e-commerce, opening their products to the world. For example using Shopify small-scale businesses can sell their products on Facebook and accept credit cards and even buy buttons for their sites for just nine dollars per month. Braintree is an affiliate of PayPal offers the service further by allowing businesses to use Venmo, PayPal, and even Bitcoin as one of their payment choices.

4. Innovating Insurance

Fintech startups have a major impact on traditional insurance structures, with a view towards creating more efficient products to small-sized business owners. The most significant change is simplifying the buying process for insurance by making it possible for business owners to buy online. The need for online insurance is likely to only increase. Although only 1 out of 4 of SMBs bought their insurance on the internet 70% of them believe likely to do so in the near future.

The attraction could be among the insurance products, which are lower in cost and are more tailored for smaller companies. For instance, insurance company Chubb has teamed up with startup Bunker to provide insurance based on use for contractors. The policies are typically customized to the duration of the work--sometimes as little as three months, and purchased through the mobile app using credit. Cost? A mere just $20 per month.

5. Expanding Retirement Options

The majority of small-scale business owners feel the pressure to compete for benefits against their larger counterparts. Making sure that retirement benefits are comparable to what employees of larger companies receive is typically a major challenge. Take into consideration that just four out of 10 employers that have less than 100 employees have retirement plans. Fintech companies are trying to alleviate this issue by reducing the benefits of these plans and making them more manageable.

For instance, Ubiquity Retirement has garnered lots of attention because it offers low-cost retirement plans designed specifically for smaller businesses. Another example is Betterment does not just help small businesses design their plans as well as provide documentation, compliance, advice and fiduciary assistance to small business owners as well as employees. Retirement benefits are exciting, however they're only one part of what's known as H.R. Tech. The field is also evolving to meet the needs of small-scale companies, offering automated solutions to manage all your benefits for employees.

Achieving the Right Fintech for Your Small Business

There's plenty of technological options to choose from. Subscribing to more than the fintech apps of a dozen does not just increase the cost of your services but also increases the likelihood that you and your team will not utilize every one of them to their fullest potential. Instead, look at your top priorities for business and search for relevant fintech solutions. For example, if managing your income has been long-term issue, consider the fintech applications designed to offer increased visibility into your finances and forecasting of income. Also, if a retirement plan is on your agenda look into fintech firms which have made benefits more affordable.

Whatever you decide to use make sure that you get your team involved. Give training on new technologies and monitor whether your business uses the product and the benefits it brings. Technology is constantly advancing to create a level playing field for small companies. Make sure you look at what Fintech can meet the needs of your business, and then use the latest technology in your favor.

The impact of Fintech

Five Methods Fintech is changing Financial Services Industry Financial Services Industry

Credit unions, banks and major financial players are trying to in the midst of new technology and software innovations, as well as advances in technology that are mainly brought about by fintech startups. This trend is fast and irreversibly altering the world's economic landscape.

The current revolution in technological advancements in finance (fintech) is expanding rapidly across the globe and has a profound impact on operations within the field which includes financial advice, customer service as well as transactions and payments as well as insurance, lending and management of accounts.

Fortunately, he summarized how disruptions caused by fintech start-ups have affected the financial industry over the few years prior and provided some data:

* 85 percent of the banks are digital transformation a priority for their business

3.3% of worldwide consumers are using fintech to transfer money

7.7% financial institutions are looking to invent more

60 percent of traditional banks will collaborate with fintech startups, and 82% anticipate these partnerships to expand in the next five years.

In the digital age in which customer-centricity is the main focus, fintech is developing solutions to better meet the needs of customers in terms of convenience, accessibility and personalization. What will the future look like in the financial industry?

Here are five ways in which fintech's revolution has reshaped the sector of financial services:

1. Omni-channel customer experience

Since digital channels continue to dominate the way that customers connect to companies, there has seen a rapid shift in interactions between users as banks have gone away from branch-based procedures and traditional operations to operate mostly in digital methods.

A seamless experience that is able to meet the demands of new customers requires mobile, social media as well as multiple channels of communication - live chat, email and SMS. The need to make it easier for customers to access communication via any medium is marking the way for businesses in their quest to create customer-centric processes.

For those who use banking the omni-channel approach means customers will experience continuous and seamless online interactions regardless of the device they are using, and offline, through "smart" branch locations that seamlessly connect to digital services. When user habits change with the advent of Fintech implies that financial institutions are becoming more sophisticated, and are planning to move sales and transactions to digital channels which assist in bringing together an better customer experience.

Fintech startups are rapidly emerging to keep up to this new trend. They will offer the technology for financial institutions to use multi-channel messaging which is paired with AI machines, machine learning and automation to improve communication between businesses and customers - an effective way to increase sales and improve customer engagement.

The current method, called co-browsing is among the most recent technologies that has been developed to assist financial services in their quest to provide omni-channel customer assistance. In addition to credit unions and banks This tool is being utilized by agents in insurance or lending companies, as well as financial advisors who are able to co-browse with clients and offer support in person.

The primary benefit of co-browsing is the fact that agents are able to navigate with customers and customers on certain websites, and step into the mix and assist with the show-and-tell approach in crucial phases of the buyer's journey starting with form filling out for pre-sales applications to post-salesales customer onboarding.

2. Chatbots for customer service

Chatbots are gaining popularity particularly among banks which use them to speed up a variety of customer interaction processes , this is why it's come to be called chat-based banking.

Agents will benefit greatly by implementing these virtual assistants. They'll spend less time dealing with basic questions and can focus on more pertinent or difficult tasks.

One of the biggest benefits that chatbot technology provides for financial services is the quick service delivery to support simple queries, directing customers to the right place (relevant websites or service departments) as well as making data collection easier.

Chatbots are also able to integrate with other technologies and applications and use machine learning to enhance their capabilities constantly. Open banking is among the innovations that will be integrated with chatbot technology to make various requests and collect pertinent financial information from customers.

From the perspective of the consumer Chatbots are useful pieces of software since - unlike human interactions , they can help all hours of the day. Virtual assistants are today always answering support questions and assisting customers to search for information on the internet in a matter of seconds, resulting in higher levels of satisfaction for customers.

Although some people prefer to use human contact for various procedures, a hybrid approach is now feasible and could soon become the new norm for financial services.

3. Open innovation to amazing innovations

The digital revolution has maintained an eye on the openness of. Financial giants are increasingly collaborating with solutions from outside and have also opened up to third party innovators to adopt new ideas and organize events.

A study from Accenture illustrates how open-concept is integrated into the approach of the various fintech firms. One real-world example could be Fidor Bank in Germany, that has developed a middleware using an open Application Programming Interface (API) that connects with existing banks' platforms to offer numerous services, including the field of lending, urgent loans, and sending money through Twitter.

Innovation that is open and accessible continues to gain popularity, creating competition as it's. Established credit unions and banks can collaborate with fintech firms that offer banking technologies accessible to simplify processes such as the assessment of affordability, credit searching and report reporting.

4. Transactions using Blockchain and cryptocurrency

In the wake of the open innovation trend there is a huge potential for companies within the financial services industry to be able to take advantage of an approach in Blockchain. Blockchain has disrupted the banking industry over the past couple of years, providing customers more efficient and lower cost methods to make transactions.

It isn't clear how this trend will influence the world, and the long-term effects however it's worth noting the way it's been implemented, and rapidly transforming the way we conduct the transfer of money and other transactions. Blockchain offers a secure trading platform with greater transparency and users are using the cryptocurrency for money transfer as well as reducing costs and reducing time.

5. Automated financial advice

Virtual assistants, also known as virtual advisors, have taken the world of financial data by storm they pose a major challenge to traditional companies. They will likely be able to prevail, however developments in automated technology for business data continue to appear and provide alternatives that are competitive.

The automation is implemented in the automated messaging system that is used through live chat as well as other channels of communication and workflows that are designed on the basis of the company's needs, and then triggered by the consumer's behavior - to boost sales and increase customer engagement. Financial guidance is typically automated, using a an approach that is a combination of humans and machines. Automation is utilized in this field extends to many procedures, from the giving of crucial advice to data-driven insight for more specific services and automated processes for onboarding customers. Automation can assist financial advisors and advisors in wealth and asset management to capture leads, develop relationships with their customers and provide a more complete services.

Fast-forward to the future

The expectations for digital banking are growing which is forcing banks to think differently about the way products and services should be offered. Equally the advancements in fintech are now covering all phases of the customer's journey using chatbots, machine-learning and AI, co-browsing, modern messaging , and automation. More developments are on the way.

The main goal for banks and financial services should remain a strategy that places the customer at the center of their business processes, ensuring the smoothest and most seamless experience.

The traditional retail banking institutions will be able to keep track of the technological revolution being led by fintech startups and other challenger players in the sector and think about possibilities for collaborations, open innovation and strategic investments that can significantly enhance their operations in accordance of the changing times.

The role in the role of Social Media and Technology in the FinTech development

The rise of social media have taken the globe to the forefront over the last decade. Facebook which is generally thought of as"the "grandfather" of the social web, established 11 years ago. YouTube the following year and Twitter two years after, according to Phil Male.

The social media are astonishing. There are currently more than 284 million Twitter users, as well as 33 millions

LinkedIn users. Yet, Facebook dwarfs them both by surpassing the 1 billion milestone last year. Furthermore, one billion people use YouTube each month.

Capitalising on social media

With such numbers it's no wonder that businesses across all sectors have been rushing to devise strategies to take advantage the benefits of using social networks as a customer and marketing communication tool. What is the case with financial services? What exactly are commercial companies doing when it comes to making use of social media for marketing?

There are specific challenges for financial companies when it comes to making use of social media as part of their customer and marketing strategies. Most important among them is the security and compliance risks, and regulations.

But, these issues aren't going to stop financial companies from implementing strategies for social media for sales, marketing as well as a the tool for providing customer services. The benefits that can be realized by businesses that utilize social media in this manner are numerous. For example, clients who interact with their bank through the internet are more likely by 12 percentage be wealthy and mass-affluent, as well as 18% more likely be in the process of becoming affluent, as per with Gallup.

This means that those who use social media are likely to rank among their most profitable financial customers. Thus, businesses that think ahead are forming strategies to figure out how they'll be able to integrate social networks into their strategy goals for the 21st century.

Chapter 11: Common applications of social media

Financial companies can make use of social media in various ways. One, obviously is to use it as a sales and marketing instrument. Financial clients of every age starting from Millennials to Matures are using social media sites to search for information on companies before deciding on which they should pursue for succeed in business. They're creating brand perceptions through comments, posts, as well as "likes" and in ways which some financial companies don't even realize.

It is essential that financial institutions be proactive, not reacting, when it comes to taking control of their online presence. However, managing interactions and comments on the social networks is just the beginning of the process when it comes to making use of social networks as a selling as well as marketing instrument.

Financial institutions that are progressive are moving beyond making use of social media as an engagement tool, to be able to participate with their customers through social media 2.0 in collecting, and utilizing the data from social networks to generate insights that can aid in marketing and sales.

For instance, these data could help financial institutions identify which finance products or services customers would like. It could also assist in determining which social media platforms are the most effective platforms to create advertisements and targeted messages. By monitoring carefully customers and prospects' post and comments on the social networks Financial organizations will gain valuable information that will give an improved understanding of their preferences for products and allows them to develop the marketing strategy.

Alongside marketing and sales, the most innovative financial companies employ social media as a crucial part of their customer-service initiatives. It's not surprising that research has shown that using social media may be is the most cost-effective method of offering customer service. For instance, handling the customer's request for assistance via social media will cost PS1 while dealing with an equivalent call costs approximately PS3.50.

Nearly half of users of social media say they should make use of it in order to obtain help from customer service. They expect the companies they work with to respond to queries regarding customer service for social media promptly: 32 percent anticipate responses within a half hour and 42 percent in one hour.

Most common social media platforms

Which financial institutions are using to communicate with their clients via social media? According to Forbes.com The winner is Twitter with 92 % of the commercial service companies that were tracked keeping an active Twitter presence. American Express is that the most active commercial service company on social media as it manages three distinct Twitter accounts and five distinct Facebook pages with 400,000 followers. AVIVA, Barclays, Charles Schwab and Chase are among the financial companies that have a strong online presence on social networks.

Many financial companies who have succeeded in implementing social media have decided to create an elaborate plan to drive their entire social strategy. The typical social strategy comprises four main elements:

1. Finding out the current online presence. The first step is to determine the current social media presence. For many organizations, particularly those with large budgets, it's larger than they think and could include many social media accounts being created on a myriad of platforms.

2. The creation of an all-encompassing, organizational-wide social media strategy for the entire organization. The strategic plan must define the manner in which social media is utilized across the entire company and connect various departments and silos which are currently working in isolation from each other. Marketing and sales may also encompass compliance with IT, human resources and customer service along with other departments.

3. Establishing social media goals and identifying the metrics needed to achieve the goals. Similar to every other organizational initiative There should be objectives and goals attached to your social media activities. They should be tangible easily tracked, measurable, and trackable and you'll be able to assess the progress your company is making in achieving them.

4. Training employees who will be to be accountable for the implementation of

this strategy. The employees shouldn't be responsible for conceiving and implementing a social strategy in the absence of being adequately educated. Social media is now an academic field according to its name, which means that we should do not invest in inadequate education to provide employees with the skills and tools they'll need to be successful.

If the last 10 years are an indication that social media isn't staying around in the future, but it will increasingly be the preferred source for financial customers as they decide on the best commercial companies to pursue succeed in business. It is therefore crucial that financial institutions devise and implement a comprehensive strategy to ensure the success of social media.

Fintech Financing

P2P Lending

Best Peer-to-Peer Lending

Peer-to peer lending allows you to be the borrower or an investor

If you aren't interested in borrowing money from a brick and mortar bank or from a traditional online lender Peer-to-peer (P2P) loans are something worth considering. The P2P loan is different from loans you've had in the past. It's not a loan from a bank, instead, but from a private group of individuals who are willing to lend money to applicants who are qualified. P2P lending sites connect investors to borrowers and lenders, as they are referred to as. Each site determines the rates and, thus the conditions (sometimes with input from investors) and allows the transaction.

P2P was only launched in 2005, however the number of rival sites has already grown to a large extent. Although they all function in the same way but they differ considerably in their qualifications, loan rates as well as the amount and duration and also in their clients. For a quick start

We scoured the internet P2P markets and came to the top five options, based on the specifics of your financial situation.

What is Peer-to-Peer lending?

The Peer to Peer (P2P) loan, often called "social" or "crowd" credit, is an alternative to financing that connects companies that want to lend money to businesses or individuals who wish to borrow money. In lieu of traditional financing, a financial technology firm (aka Fintech) creates a website platform that connects lenders directly with loan applicants.

The terms and rates you pay (and the likelihood of you being eligible in your first year of eligibility) remain based on the same aspects that other lenders take into consideration. For example you credit score, history of credit and income all have a significant impact on the likelihood of you being able to get P2P loans, and that is, in turn, the price you pay for the loan, regardless of what you're performing. If you have excellent credit with a good income, as well as a high DTI ratio and you're able to find the most reasonable price on P2P loans. If you're suffering from issues with credit or other financial issues, obtaining the best loan deal (or even getting a credit approval) may be a problem.

What is Peer-to-Peer lending?

If you are applying for a loan through P2P The process typically includes the following steps.

The applicant must complete and submit an online application. This process will typically include an inquiry about credit, whether hard or soft.

The lending platform could assign you a risk classification or grade. Your rating can affect the interest rate and the terms you're given. If you're happy with your idea, you'll want to proceed.

Investors review your loan request. It is important to include information about how you intend to spend the money or explain why lending money to you is an acceptable risk. Your tale could increase the likelihood of getting funds. Based on the way in which your P2P platform is constructed lenders can offer bids to acquire your business. But, the loan request could also be rejected.

You agree to the loan. If an investor puts in an offer that you are happy with, you'll go over the conditions and accept the loan. On the platform, money could get deposited in your checking account within a few hours due to the week or day of the week.

Pay your monthly bills. In general, P2P lenders report accounts to credit bureaus in the same way as traditional lenders, so late payments can harm the credit rating. In addition, late payments could result in charges for late payments that can raise the overall expense of borrowing.

Different types of loans are available through Peer-to-Peer Loans

P2P loans are typically utilized for a variety of similar purpose to personal loans. Here are some of the loan types that you can discover on the popular P2P sites.

* Personal Loans

*Home Improvement Loans

* Auto Loans

* Student Loans

* Medical Loans

* Business Credit

* The investing Side in Peer-to-Peer Lending

P2P lending may assist investors in earning extra earnings and broaden their portfolios. P2P investing can be appealing to many individuals who want to build their savings for their benefit. If all goes as planned P2P investors can enjoy higher returns on their savings than what they can earn through an account with a high yield or the certificate of deposit (CD) or other types of investments.

Being an P2P investor begins by the application to open an account with the P2P loan platform. If you're accepted, you make deposits to be distributed via the platform to eligible customers. The loan request will be reviewed (along with the risk grade of the applicant) and select the ones you'd like to approve by providing the complete amount to be lent or just a portion of it. On your account, you'll be able to track your principal earnings and interest, as your borrowers make repayments. You'll be able to live the earnings (you'll likely have to pay tax on these) or reinvest them.

Remember that there's risks involved in any investment. It's true that there's no guarantee your borrower will repay the amount stated (whether the platform pursues the delinquents and, to what extent are some issues to in advance).

There's also the possibility that the lending service itself might shut down. In either scenario you may be able to lose a substantial part of your investment particularly if the loan that you took out was unsecure.

Do you think that Peer-to-Peer lending is the right fit?

A P2P loan might be a perfect fit for those who aren't able to qualify with traditional lenders or prefer to look at other financing options. However, keep in mind that despite the technological advancements the process of obtaining a P2P loan is not that different from the standard one. The most creditworthy applicants are typically eligible for the lowest rates and the best conditions. The effort to build credit could be in your favor. While you're at it, looking around for the least complicated P2P deal can help in saving money.

The advantages and disadvantages of peer to peer lending

Peer-to-peer lending has a number of advantages for both borrowers and lenders:

Better returns for investors The P2P loan typically offers greater returns for investors than other kinds of investments.

Accessible source of funding for a handful of individuals, peer-to peer lending might be a more suitable source of funding than traditional credit from institutions. This could be due to the poor credit score of the borrower, or the unusual reason for the loan.

Lower interest ratesfor P2P loans typically come with lower interest rates because of the greater competition among lenders and the lower fees for origination.

Some disadvantages

However, it comes with a few drawbacks:

Credit risk: Loans made through peer-to-peer are subject to high credit risk. A lot of borrowers who seek P2P loans have poor credit scores, which don't permit them to obtain a typical loan from banks. Thus, the lender must keep in mind the probability of default of their counterpart.

The government doesn't offer insurance or provide any protection to the lenders in the event in the event of a borrower's default.

Legislation: Certain jurisdictions do not permit peer-to-peer lending, or require companies which offer such services to conform to regulations governing investment. So, peer-to peer lending may not be accessible to certain customers or lenders.

Five reasons P2P lending is the best option for small-sized enterprises.

1. It is more likely to understand your requirements P2P lending operates in an approach that is very unlike traditional banks. A SME is trying to get the loan of banks or financial institution to access. In contrast with P2P lending and SME, he is

required to put his requirements in a simple and then thousands of private lenders are able to examine. If you've got a decent credit rating, chances are that you'll be offered multiple offers to finance.

2. Speed - Small and medium-sized businesses often have the issue of flow of funds and must urgently be able to cover a shortage of capital or cash. Traditional methods of obtaining loans are lengthy complicated, time-consuming, and cumbersome and require multiple documents and may take the duration of days. After a borrower's profile has been accepted, getting a P2P loan sanctioned and ultimately receiving the money could be as quick as few hours. The credit rating process and background check of the borrower are light years faster in comparison.

3. No collateral - SMB typically have a difficult time when it comes to offering an assurance for loans. This is typically true for SMBs in the service sector. Banks are

often reluctant to approve business loans without collateral This suggests that an overwhelming majority of SMBs are unable to use their assets for business loans. P2P lending on the other one hand does not require collateral or security and can be obtained with minimal hassle. A good credit score and, as a result the capacity to pay on behalf of entrepreneurs or the company is essential.

4. Lower costs P2P loans are more transparent and have no hidden costs. Most of the time, SMEs discover some unpleasant conditions after signing the loan agreement. A P2P loan with an honest company is typically clear and has no unexpected surprises. P2P loans are also very flexible in the case of the prepayment of loans since there's no upfront or one-time payment fees. For instance, all the details are clearly explained on our website and clients receive a statements of accounts.

5. The future - The majority of the current method of financing or raising funds has been in place for a number of years without much or any innovation. The needs of an SME present a different set of requirements and in an era of globalization, finance hasn't kept up with changing requirements. In this scenario, P2P loans provide a more transparent, less expensive, quicker and more modern solution for financing business. P2P loans are the most efficient use of technology as well as traditional lending strategies to come to a single option that has proven.

Tips to Borrow

i. There are some basic guidelines that every prospective borrower should be sure to follow to receive their loan.

ii. Be honest with yourself - look at yourself as the lender would. You'll want for the loan provider to believe that you're type of person who will pay back any loan, so show proof and emphasize your creditworthiness.

iii. Be honest with the lender Never mislead or deceive. The internet is a loan community. So you shouldn't create reputations for fraud. If you've faced issues with your credit or finances in the past, make it clear. It's better to disclose your past rather than being caught lying.

iv. Layout Your Case - Discuss what you're planning to do with the money. Particularly, explain how the funds are going to be used, and refrain from vague claims. Lenders don't like vagueness.

v. Neatness is Important Make sure you proofread your application to ensure that you have the spelling and grammar right. Nothing says scammer or stupid like type of a careless or poorly-written use. You must have the confidence of lenders and they must be able to trust their money to an honest borrower.

vi. Don't exceed the limit - Lenders will look at your debt-to-income ratio prior to granting you the loan. If your application does not show any income streams or a credit history that is conducive to repaying, it's likely you'll be granted the loan you've requested. Be sure to make reasonable requests.

Crowdfunding

In the latter half of 2000 there was a fourth option that became an option for those looking to get an idea to get off the ground by crowdfunding. It could be because of raising funds from a huge number of people. A large number of people gather small investments from individuals to provide the capital to push a company or project off the ground. Individuals and charities as well as companies can organize a campaign for certain causes. Anyone is able to contribute.

Crowdfunding in a Snap

Crowdfunding is a way of raising capital via the efforts of family members, friends customers, as well as individual investors. This approach taps into the joint efforts of an outsized pool of individuals--primarily online via social media and crowdfunding platforms--and leverages their networks for greater reach and exposure.

Different types of Crowdfunding

A. Securities-based Crowdfunding gives the opportunity for individuals to buy shares in privately-owned corporations (aka startups). In this type of program, investors get the promise of stocks future shares, other securities that the company issues as a payment for equity. This article will focus on Equity-based Crowdfunding. However, there are many different kinds of Crowdfunding. These include:

B. Donation-based Crowdfunding occurs when a person makes a donation to a chosen project or cause (think GoFundMe).

C. Reward-based Crowdfunding works as it sounds like. People make donations to unlock the reward of their choice that is linked to the cause they are supporting. For example, you could perhaps help to fund a new line, and then receive the product back in exchange.

D. Peer-to peer lending allows people to borrow money directly from other people without the need of a bank or financial institution acting as a middleman. Think of it as crowdfunding for debt.

It is. A. Real estate crowdfunding gives people the chance to invest in on projects in the inland. It can be particularly beneficial for those who are interested in investing in land but who don't want to harm the mortgage brokers, land agents or contractors. It's usually a specific kind of crowdfunding for securities.

F. Crowdfunding for human capital could be a method for individuals to raise funds to fund their own personal development or to fund projects. Investors have the chance to finance an idea by securing a percentage of the prize. In this case there are many poker players who are able to crowdfund their money for playing and then give a portion the winnings back to investors.

Which type of crowdfunding is the best for your small Business?

You're planning to use an injection of cash to boost your small-scale company, but you're not sure that you'll qualify for a typical smaller commercial loan. Are you in the market to win the lottery (or taking out your savings) What other options do you have to fund your business? Crowdfunding might be the right option an option for those who are.

If you're unfamiliar with the concept, Crowdfunding basically lets you fund your company through a pool of people who wish to be part of a community that shares your activities. Depending on the type of

Crowdfunding that you decide to use and the amount you'll have to pay back the loan or offer incentives to investors who contribute to your campaign.

Four kinds of Crowdfunding

If you're convinced of the idea of raising money this way then you'll realize that you have two choices. Certain, one of them will speak to you much more clearly than the other.

1. Crowdfunding for debt

Similar to a typical credit card, debt-based crowdfunding is the raising of money which you then pay back. One of the most well-known examples is Kiva. While Kiva is known for its focus on aiding entrepreneurs in developing nations however, it is also accessible to U.S.-based business owners.

A benefit of platforms like Kiva has been that they typically do not require the same criteria to approve a borrower as a bank does. They don't care about your credit score rather than the sector you're in as well as the length of time you've been operating for and the degree of risk you pose to lenders. The larger the loan that you want to get the higher the requirements you'll need to satisfy.

2. Equity crowdfunding

Another option for crowdfunding is to give shareholders equity shares of your company. It's similar to obtaining angel investment as well as risk capital but more manageable when you're willing to incorporate it an effort in the marketing process to let people know about your campaign.

Wefunder is a good instance of equity-based crowdfunding. It is home to for every type of business, from the cafe in the corner to the biotech business that is examining the benefits of cultivating plants. There are many options to choose the equity that someone can receive as a reward for investing however, the stocks (with as well as not dividends) and convertible notes are a possibility.

The benefit is that you can set the conditions for the amount of equity you're willing offer up. You don't have to repay a loan. However, there are some drawbacks. very few people are aware of equity crowdfunding vs alternatives, because it's still relatively new. You'll be able to get investors to sign up through the various crowdfunding options.

3. Reward-based Crowdfunding

The second type of Crowdfunding is fascinating as, instead of returning funds or inviting others to take a stake in the organization You're rewarding donors with rewards. It could be as easy as sending a thank you card for a small amount. This could also include providing the opportunity to access your product earlier or even flying out the top contributor for an exclusive day out with your business.

You've probably heard about Kickstarter which has 10 million users who have contributed to projects on the site (maybe you're one of those). If you're looking for money to fund the development of your game on a computer, write your feminist book or launch your eco-friendly shoes or anything else, anyone who finds your campaign appealing is able to contribute. The advantages of Crowdfunding based on rewards are that you don't have to repay a loan as well as your supporters who will be the only ones to have access to your item should be quite enthusiastic to share the news about the product. However, there is lots of pressure to increase funds in a short time and it could be a bit overwhelming to solicit small or even $10 donations once you're in need of the big bucks.

4. Donor crowdfunding

The last option to think about is crowdfunding for donors. This type of crowdfunding is a good option because there is no requirement to repay the money or give incentives to the donors. GoFundMe is an extremely well-known crowdfunding tool based on donations.

The attraction is not having to make payments and you can put the money into a figure for your company. If there's a drawback that you'll face, it's that sites such as GoFundMe are mostly used to raise money for personal reasons. Thus, it's possible that donors won't have the intention of supporting businesses via these channels.

Chapter 12: What do you want to know? like to know

Whichever type of Crowdfunding that you choose is the best option for your business, you must remember that the success of your campaign will be contingent completely on the power of marketing you put to it. Donors and investors love an authentic story. The way to tell your story is through your project's web page and a short video and through outreach on blogs, social media or email, as well as every other avenue that is possible.

It's probably the most unnoticed aspect of Crowdfunding that is not being considered by companies. Some business owners think it's simple money. They post their project only to be disappointed when they don't see the money. Like everything else you'd like to offer you must plug it. It's up to you to convince people to give up their cash (with no guarantee that they'll get any repayments or other rewards). You must convince people to believe that your company can be worth their time. A few business owners engage crowdfunding marketing experts to ensure the success of their crowdfunding campaign.

If you're able to take the effort of spreading the public about your campaign, Crowdfunding can be usually a great resource whether you're trying to introduce a new product, looking to increase operations, or simply looking to increase the number of people who are your crowd.

What are the benefits of Crowdfunding for businesses?

As with other companies business can utilize Crowdfunding as a way to increase the capital of their venture. When we talk about Crowdfunding as a business, we usually think that it is a form of angel investment, start-ups as well as transactions outside of conventional financial institution. Crowdfunding in business offers the perfect opportunity for startups to access a large number of investors effectively.

What are the benefits of Crowdfunding to businesses?

Platforms such as Republic make it possible for investors (or supporters or backers, as they're commonly referred to) to sign up for a campaign by just a couple of clicks. Most crowdfunding campaigns are based on a collective objective and provide incentives to the people who invest. When the objective is achieved then the investors usually appreciate backing the campaign. If the corporation will be exiting in the next few years, such as an acquisition or the initial public offering, supporters are able to earn cash or share.

What makes Crowdfunding different?

With Crowdfunding, many investors are invited to join and share a portion in the profits. It's usually a major departure from traditional fundraising where businesses or institutions look for money from one or few significant investors. Crowdfunding is also primarily conducted on the internet, while other kinds of funding are mostly done offline.

The advantages of Crowdfunding

The benefits of Crowdfunding extend far beyond the simple act of raising funds.

Accessing capital is the main reason for startups. A lot of early-stage companies are not considered by VCs due to a variety of reasons. Getting cash from banks or even productive relationships are not effective methods. Crowdfunding can level the playing field by reducing the reliance on traditional and occasionally exclusive fundraising strategies. Crowdfunding campaigns are also distinct in their capacity to generate interest from potential customers and boost engagement. Since you must involve everyone involved to make a difference the campaigns are a wonderful opportunity to increase awareness of the company, brand product or service. The goal of the campaign and its timeframe create an atmosphere of urgency that entices investors. This provides startups with the opportunity to create excitement and attract early adopters. Startups are able to reach potential customers, who can also serve as investors or brand ambassadors. Successful campaigns prove that there is a demand for an item, and also provides the necessary runway to help the development of new projects.

From an investor's point of view Crowdfunding is a straightforward thank you to fund projects as well as other individuals who you truly believe in and are concerned about. In addition, it allows investors to invest smaller amount of positions in several ventures, which allows them to diversify their portfolios, and increasing the chances of a huge payout.

However, it is an investment that is high-risk, investors should invest only in capital, they are comfortable losing. The only thing the investor requires is one big blockbuster investment in order to recover the losses of other investments and earn an unimaginably high yield.

The dangers of crowdfunding

From a business's point of view Crowdfunding can be a great option due to the speed at which it can raise funds. Although it takes a lot of effort, marketing and attention for an effective crowdfunding campaign, more than 90% of startups on Republic have been successful in raising funds. Although it's not 100% guaranteed, platforms such as the Republic make use of every resource available to increase awareness for each campaign.

Strategies for crowdfunding success

How do you get the most out of future crowdfunding opportunities?

The aim is to find out the purposes for which funds will be allocated by the company or person that is hosting the campaign.

Teamwork is essential to increase the chance that the company will be successful. Examining the founders' advisors, founders and the history of the team could be a great method to determine whether the founder has appropriate people to carry out the tasks they're setting the foundation for the coming years.

It is the UVP (unique value-added proposition) -- make sure to look for companies employing technology in a unique or unique method, or which could likely alter an existing market. Try to determine their UVP to determine the uniqueness of their approach and verify that they provide an open and distinctive product to their market.

Find out the market's traction and research for the product or service will be just right if there's a lot of demand from potential buyers. Find out how they intend to conquer. Are there any requirements for their product or is there room for expansion? You can also look up the company's market share for information about how their idea performs in its initial markets.

Fraud is a real threat. Always look at the website of the company, the filings, and other documentation to make sure that they're authentic. Do not just click the next link that pops up via social media.

What can small-scale businesses gain from Crowdfunding?

Capital

There's a chance that you didn't have the amount of money for your business idea in the way you expected. It's just a bit more time to come up with your visionary idea. What do you do? You might want to explore Crowdfunding for the extra money. If your idea and the style appeal to people that like it, it will attract not just attention, but lots of money that can assist in making that idea a reality and into the hands of consumers.

This approach won't need you to be to be able to access the entirety of your business equity and you'll never accumulate debt in the process. Of course, you'll want to present donors with gifts, and make them the first to receive the item once it's ready to be shipped.

It can be used as a symbol for the idea

Prior to making a sacrifice of your savings and taking out loans based on an idea that could or may not be successful in the long run, you'll present the idea to the public. It's not even a good idea to know how that the market will react to your concept until it's out there. Alternatively, through Crowdfunding, you'll get feedback prior to committing your funds. Once you begin to gather money from your supporters it could provide you with confirmation that your idea is worthy of pursuing and introduce it to the marketplace.

Marketing

New ideas and new products got to be marketed and introduced to the audience-cultivating awareness. Consider Crowdfunding as the initial marketing stage, the first step in introducing your product. Create a fan base prior to launching your product. People who have pledged their money to the success of your venture will be watching your progress over time and will mention it in their circle of contacts.

Even if you do not meet your goal for funding but you'll still be able to observe how consumers respond to your brand new product.

Mitigates Financial Risk

With Crowdfunding, you're not placing your company, or your assets in jeopardy. When you take out loans from banks, they will have to be repaid with interest. Bringing in investors can cause you to forfeit your business equity.

If your venture doesn't perform or doesn't make money there will be problems with repaying the money you borrowed, which is a risky venture. Crowdfunding involves sourcing revenue through willing individuals who support your concept and want you to succeed.

Collect Comments

The idea you are presenting on crowdfunding sites lets you gather valuable feedback from your customers. Your crowd, while helping your cause financially, could also provide valuable feedback that can help you improve your concept.

When you go through the process you'll miss certain crucial aspects of the design.

All over the globe are eager to share their opinions and ideas about what they enjoy about the concept, and how it can be changed in the future.

It's not expensive

Crowdfunding doesn't cost you a penny. Some crowdfunding sites take a certain percent of the money you've collected however they don't charge any fees in advance.

You've got everything you need to achieve but you have nothing to lose when you decide to crowdfund your business. You'll even be prepared to raise ALL the capital needed to develop your business idea without any sacrifices in your pockets.

Cryptocurrency

How do you define cryptocurrency?

The term "cryptocurrency" can refer to a form of payment that can be traded online for products or services. Numerous companies have issued their own currencies which are often referred to as tokens and they are usually traded in exchange for the top or service the company offers. You can think of them as arcade chips or casino tokens. You'll be able to exchange actual currency to use the fantastic or service.

The technology used to create cryptocurrencies is known as the blockchain. Blockchain could be described as a decentralised system that can be found on numerous computers to records and manage transactions. The main reason people are attracted to the use of blockchain lies in its safety.

A virtual or digital currency secured with cryptography makes it virtually impossible to duplicate or counterfeit. Many cryptocurrency are decentralised networks that are backed by blockchain technology, a distributed ledger that is enforced by a diverse computer network. The most notable characteristic of cryptocurrencies is that they're not created by a central government agency, making them theoretically invulnerable to manipulation by the government or government.

The most important takeaways

A cryptocurrency can be described as an entirely new type of digital asset that is supported by a network which is spread over a vast amount of computers. The decentralised structure of the cryptocurrency lets them operate outside the control of governments or central authorities.

The term "cryptocurrency" originates from encryption methods that are employed to safeguard the network.

Blockchains are methods to ensure the authenticity of data transactional and are essential to the numerous cryptocurrency.

There are many experts who believe blockchain technology could disrupt several sectors, including finance and law.

Cryptocurrencies are criticized for a variety of reasons, such as their use in illegal activities and volatility in exchange rates and the vulnerabilities of the infrastructure that supports them. They have also been acknowledged for their portability, divisibility, inflation resistance and their transparency.

Understanding Cryptocurrencies

Cryptocurrencies are systems that allow secure transactions online, based on the concept that of digital "tokens," which are recorded in the ledger as entries within the system. "Crypto" means various encryption algorithms and cryptographic methods which protect these entries such as elliptical curve encryption public-private key pair, and hashing functions.

Different types of cryptocurrency

The first cryptocurrency based on blockchain technology was Bitcoin and it is still the most popular and expensive. Nowadays, there are a myriad of other cryptocurrencies, each with different capabilities and specifications. Some of them are forks or clones of Bitcoin and other are brand new currencies that were created from scratch.

Bitcoin

The only and the most well-known and primary cryptocurrency. Bitcoin is a digital gold standard within the whole cryptocurrency-industry, is employed as a worldwide means of payment, and is that the de-facto currency of cyber-crime like darknet markets or ransomware. In the past seven years the price of Bitcoin has grown from zero to nearly 700 dollars and its volume of transactions has reached 200.000 every day.

There's not much more to say to mention - Bitcoin will not go away.

Ethereum

The idea of young crypto-geek Vitalik Buterin, who is now in second place in the hierarchy of cryptocurrency. Apart from Bitcoin the blockchain of ethereum doesn't just validate a set of balances and accounts, but of states. It implies that Ethereum can't only handle transactions but also more complicated contracts and software.

This flexibility allows Ethereum an ideal instrument for the blockchain-related application. However, it comes with an expense. Following an incident known as the Hack of the DAO which is an Ethereum smart contract that is based on Ethereum The developers decided to pursue make a difficult fork with no consensus and resulted in the creation of Ethereum Classic. Apart from that there are a variety of variations of Ethereum and Ethereum is the host for several Tokens such as DigixDAO or Augur. This makes Ethereum an assortment of cryptocurrency families more than just one currency.

Ripple

Although Ripple offers its own cryptocurrency, XRP but it's a couple of platforms that can handle IOUs. The currency XRP isn't used as a means for storing value or exchange but rather as an instrument to protect the system from spam.

Ripple is, in contrast to Bitcoin and Ethereum, is no mining because all coins have been pre-mined. Ripple has proven to be a huge asset in the commercial market because a lot of banks have joined the Ripple network.

Litecoin

Litecoin is one of the main cryptocurrency that came following Bitcoin and was known as such as silver because it was bitcoin, the digital gold. More efficient than bitcoin, with the largest quantity of tokens and a new mining algorithm, Litecoin was an amazing breakthrough, designed specifically to function as the less expensive brother of bitcoin. "It enabled the development of various other cryptocurrency that used its codebase, but it made it even light. " Examples include Dogecoin as well as Feathercoin.

Although Litecoin was unable to find any real-world application and was relegated to second place in the market after bitcoin, it's active in its development and trading and stored to act as a backup option in the event that Bitcoin is unable to meet its goals.

Monero

Monero is the largest and most famous illustration that demonstrates this CryptoNight algorithm. The algorithm was created to provide the security features that Bitcoin isn't able to provide. If you use Bitcoin each transaction is recorded on the blockchain, which means the transaction trail is frequently tracked. When the idea of ring-signatures was introduced, the concept of ring-signatures CryptoNight

CryptoNight algorithm was made ready to follow this trail.

The initial version of CryptoNight, Bytecoin, was slow and was therefore dismissed in the eyes of the general public. Monero was the first non-pre minedversion, similar to bitcoin, and generated tons of consciousness. There are many other versions of cryptocurrency with their minor advancements but none was ever as popular as Monero.

Monero's popularity soared in the summer of 2016 when darknet marketplaces decided to accept it as a currency. The result was a steady growth in its price, however, the specific use of Monero is still surprisingly tiny. Beyond that several cryptocurrencies, there are many others from a variety of families. Most of them are nothing quite attempts to succeed in investors and quickly make money, but tons of them promise playgrounds to check innovations in cryptocurrency-technology.

Benefits and disadvantages of cryptocurrency

Benefits

They are a way of making it easier to transfer money directly between two parties without the need for an untrustworthy third party like of banking institution or MasterCard company. Transfers are secured with the help of private and public keys, as well as various incentive mechanisms, such as Proof of Work and Proof of Stake.

In modern crypto systems users "wallet," or account address, has an public key. However, the private key is exclusive to the person who owns it and is used to verify transactions. Transfers are processed with no processing costs which allows users to avoid paying the high charges that are charged by banks and financial institutions to process wire transfers.

Advantages

The nature of cryptography as semi-anonymous transactions allows them to be used for a range of illicit activities such as evasion and concealment. However, many cryptocurrency enthusiasts are adamant about their privacy and cite the advantages of privacy such as protection for whistleblowers and activists under oppressive government. Certain cryptos are more private than others.

For instance, Bitcoin may be a rather unwise choice to conduct illegal transactions online, because the investigation of Bitcoin blockchain has allowed authorities in bringing charges against criminals. However, more secure coins are available, such as Dash, Monero, or ZCash and are more difficult to track.

Criticisms of cryptocurrency

Because the advertising costs associated with digital currencies are covered flexible and on demand that the rate of the way that cryptographic currency is frequently traded for cash is subject to a wide range of. The arrangement of various digital payment methods guarantees the full extent of the shortfall.

Bitcoin witnessed a series of sudden surges and then a sharp decline in value, increasing to upwards to as high as $19,000 for Bitcoin in December. of 2017 only to drop to $7,000 over the next few months. The cryptocurrency market is considered by some economists as an extremely short-lived trend or speculative bubble.

There's the concern that cryptocurrencies such as Bitcoin do not have any connection to tangible products. However, some research has found that the value of producing a Bitcoin that requires more and more electricity, directly linked with its value in the market. Blockchains are extremely secure, but other components of the cryptocurrency ecosystem, like wallets and exchanges aren't immune to hackers. Since the beginning of Bitcoin's existence, numerous transactions online have been the subject of theft and hacking and often involving a lot of dollars worth of "coins" taken. Many observers consider the potential benefits of cryptocurrencies in the same way as they can protect their value from inflation and facilitating exchange, while also being easier to divide and move than precious metals , and remaining free of the sway of central banks as well as governments.

What are the advantages of accepting cryptocurrency for small Businesses?

1. Attracting New Customers

Smaller businesses can increase their customer base by incorporating a cryptocurrency-based system to their payment options. According to a poll that showed 39% of the population would prefer the use of bitcoin as a method of payment for purchases of all kinds.

Low Cost for Transaction

Transaction costs are often an impact on business profits and won't be lowered. Because cryptocurrency is decentralised, and not having a regulatory body there is no fee. Furthermore, transactions are faster than bank transfers that are regular.

Protecting against Chargebacks and Frauds by Curbing

Secure payment could be a game changer in the realm of digital payment. Cryptocurrency is backed by blockchain technology, so transactions are irrevocable and cannot be reversed. The money is added directly to the blockchain through mining, and trades cannot be altered.

Cryptocurrency does not offer loans or debt. The concept is not even existent. It is impossible to spend money that you do not have. It stops fraud as well as chargebacks, which makes transactions much clearer and more simple.

Global Access and Sales Growth

Small-scale businesses can grow and expand their reach to buyers from abroad for whom their products or services were once unattainable. The crypto will be credited by the decentralised nature of crypto.

It has the possibility to be a currency that is worldwide as there are no limitations to your business's digital assets. Crypto has removed the hurdles of cash flow across the globe, such as waiting for the processing of international transactions, as well as the high cost in exchange rates.

Brand Image

When you announce that your company accepts cryptocurrency, it helps you to establish your business apart from the competition. Cryptocurrency also has a dedicated community of customers who insist to purchase from or support businesses that accept this payment method.

What can your business do to accept the use of cryptocurrency?

To be able to use cryptocurrency, you'll need an electronic wallet or wallet that holds keys for public and private keys. Unique identifiers indicate ownership of tokens.

What is Digital Wallets?

They can be hardware wallets or software wallets that, like traditional banks can be used to hold and trade. Market makers can participate in the cryptocurrency trading market and store these digital funds.

Making transactions with these currencies involves significant transaction fees that these digital wallets are charged. Customers aren't yet ready to use their digital wallets directly. The companies that manage these digital wallets will become third-party and have the responsibility of the cryptocurrency of the customer.

Which Digital Wallets do need to choose from?

Numerous start-ups such as Crypto.com, Coinbase, and TenX offer platforms where market makers are able to trade and make use of the digital currency.

The digital wallets are in contradiction to the whole concept of cryptocurrency which states that there is no involvement by an outside party.' We agree that these businesses provide an additional layer of secure and efficient transactions and provide a straightforward connection.

Other businesses, such as XanPool have done well to provide quick and non-custodial solutions for transactions in cryptocurrency. This means that customers can transfer money instantly to each other bank, while the software of the company guarantees the immediate delivery of the trade. This means that the money does not actually come into the company's custody. This system of custody-free transactions can provide both users and consequently, the business itself. Businesses can also join these wallets online and use as gateways.

Neo as well as challenger banks

Neobank is a digital-only banks without physical branches. They operate under an approved bank license in the market. The banks offer mobile and digital financial solutions for payment such as remittances, money transfers and remittances services as well as lending, checking and saving accounts, insurance and mortgages exclusively through mobile apps. Neobanks also offer added value services such as automated accounting, expense management, payroll, especially for growing small and medium-sized businesses.

The Challenger banks are established companies and have a complete banking license in the market. They provide banks offer services such as loans, savings and investments accounts, merchant and checking accounts credit cards for mobile, mobile banking mobile banking, etc. (retirement savings insurance, as well as trading in and buying of cryptocurrency). (retirement savings, insurance products, and buying and selling of cryptocurrency). banks continue to challenge the traditional banks by innovating and by incorporating various technologies into their offerings.

Together, the challenger and neo banks have joined the banking system, offering advanced features, real-time solutions and customer-centric products and services. These are posing challenges to traditional banks in the market.

The higher interest rates that are offered to clients over conventional banks as well as government and regulatory support for banking operations, and the improved access to mobile banking are the main drivers in the development of this market. However, the difficulty of acquiring customers online and the profitability of the start-up banks hinder market expansion. Additionally, the neo and challenger banking market is expected to provide lucrative opportunities for banks to expand their operations by enhancing their online offerings to the unbanked population of emerging economies. In addition, expanding business as well as the expansion of existing portfolios of banks and bundling their merchandise offerings, and providing custom solutions are another key sector for these Fintech banks in the coming years.

The neo as well as challenger bank market is divided based on the concept of service type as well as the end-user and the region. For the purpose of type of service it is classified into mobile banking, loans as well as checking and bank accounts and payment and money transfer, and so on. For the user, it's divided into private and business. In terms of geography, it's studied across North America, Europe, Asia-Pacific and LAMEA.

The main players that are profiled in the global neo and challenger banks market research include Atom Bank plc, Fidor Solutions AG, Monzo Bank Limited, Movencorp, Inc., MYbank, Number26 GmbH, Simple Finance Technology Corporation, Tandem Bank, UBank limited, and WeBank. They have used a variety of strategies to increase their reach and increase their standing within the market.

Benefits for stakeholders that are important

The study offers a comprehensive study of the global challenger and neo bank markets together with future and present developments to understand the coming investment pockets. The study provides information on the main factors, constraints and opportunities, as well as their impact on market's size is offered.

Porter's Five Forces analysis demonstrates the power of buyers and suppliers working within the industry. The quantitative analysis of the global challenger and neo bank markets between 2020 and 2027 is presented to figure out the potential of the market.

The Blueprint for Challenger Bank. Challenger Bank

In summarising the ever-changing requirements of the consumer, the absence of financial wellness assistance from banks as well as open banking policies of governments around the globe (discussed in the future) and, consequently the rise of mobile banking There are two key elements that are missing from developing new challenger banks technological infrastructure and. Two options are that offer a combination of both of these components: Banking-as-a Service (BaaS) partnerships or the direct connection directly with a bank.

The Banking-as a-Service model has evolved into a powerful option in FinTech to help bring a more customer-centric bank to the market swiftly digitally. BaaS providers are able to establish banks with a banking infrastructure using APIs (application programming interfaces) that can be available and operational within months, without commercial licenses (for most uses) or major capital rounds. APIs are often portrayed in terms of Lego blocks that are joined to create a bank's core via the API's calls the user's profile and account are typically created, and transactions are completed. Then, further customization is added on top of that to set up direct deposit, open-end credit cards as well as credit cards. They also ease the processing of loans. The calls will be synced with an institution that is the person who holds the funds and accounts. A few examples of BaaS platforms include Synapse, Cambr, Bankable and Treezor.

The other option could be the direct-to-bank integration. Numerous banks across the globe have entered into collaboration with fintech companies or even created their own BaaS-type platforms in distinct divisions. In the same way, APIs are wont to facilitate customer-initiated account onboarding, financing, and various other banking transactions. Neobanks be more accountable for creating compliance with regard to implementation, as well as user assistance when integrating to banks directly. The timeframe for approval, integration and launch is usually longer, too. A few examples of the top banks that are involved in this include BBVA, Fidor Bank, and GreenDot.

There's a lesser-known option of the FinTech firm obtaining proper licenses (or commercial charters for banks) independently, to establish independent banks from beginning to end. Once they are approved and operating, a few of these challenger banks are now ready to license their own proprietary systems to regional banks as well as other FinTechs that are seeking innovative banking.

What's the Future of Challenger Banks

The Fintech challengers are slowly taking away relationships with banks for many years. In addition to the ones which are truly challenger banks and non-bank names such as PayPal, Venmo, Mint as well as Rocket Mortgage offer customers easy methods to make payments and understand their financials and be approved for loan to finance home equity. These businesses are known for processing mobile cards and e-commerce has to be approved for partnerships or charters in banking and new companies outside of the normal banking world offer similar services, creating an alternative sector to the banks which have been transformed into banks.

Beyond the standard banking options (of an account with a time deposit as well as debit card payment options) The world will begin to specialize in specialized features offered by specific segments in 2020:

Freelancers require extra assistance in taxes, tax withholding as well as employee benefits.

Immigrants -- help in opening accounts quickly online for newcomers and gaining access to credit and savings;

Small businesses -- help is required to manage the balance sheet, including cost monitoring

Minor/kids is an educational bank that helps you learn how to budget effectively save, build, and credit

Seniors and 'at-risk' adults • individualized support for access via an attorney's power custodianship and family trusts and savings and wealth preservation retirement benefits, health care;

Travelers -- the ability to make use of a worldwide account and credit card without any additional charges or restrictions.

Key market segments

By Service Type

* Loans

* Mobile Banking

* Bank account and checking account

* Money Transfer, Payment and Money

* Other

By the user

* Business

* Personal

By Region

* North America

* U.S.

* Canada

* Europe

* UK

* Germany

* France

* Italy

* Spain

* Netherlands

* Nordic Countries

* Other regions of Europe

* Asia-Pacific

* China

* Japan

* South Korea

* India

* Australia

* Singapore

* Other regions of Asia-Pacific

* LAMEA

* Latin America

* Middle East

* Africa

Key Market Players

* Atom Bank plc

* Fidor Solutions AG

* Monzo Bank Limited

* Movencorp, Inc.

* MYbank

* Number26 GmbH

* Simple Finance Technology Corporation

* Tandem Bank

* UBank limited

* WeBank

If you've been keeping an eye on fintech trends and trends, you'll think that "neo banks and "challenger banks are being hailed as the source of the next thing to happen in this era. From the looks of things, they're likely to stay.

How are new banks disrupting the banking for business situation?

If you are hearing this for the very first time Neo banks are digital banks without physical presence. They connect with customers through mobile apps and online platforms.

First wave of Neo banks made their debut in the early part of 2010, with Monzo along with Atom Bank. Other top neo-clanks to hit markets later included Chime, Simple, Starling, N26, Moven, and Volt. These banks simplify banking for start-ups and SMEs by:

It provides them with a platform that includes a business accounting feature as the core of the product; and additional features of value, such as expense management as well as automated payroll, and accounting. It is centered around it.

We offer features that provide solutions to the specific business finance challenges encountered by SMEs.

Conclusion

Thank you so much for purchasing this book!

I hope this book has been useful in helping you comprehend the many aspects in financial technology.

It is the next stage applying what you have learned from this book.

Thank you!